The commemorative liquidambar tree, autumn 2016

Girls in crocodile, 1920s

The Dutch garden showing the intact Camellia walk

Recently planted bed in the Dutch garden

SCHOOLGIRL DAYS AT

MILTON MOUNT COLLEGE

1920–1960

"Prayer and Work" – the School Motto

The Miltonian Guild

First published in 2016

Copyright

© The Miltonian Guild and the Milton Mount Foundation

ISBN 9780993532207

Sub-editor: Martin Neal
Cover design by Alan Formby-Jackson

Printed by
Sherwood PF Ltd Nottingham

ACKNOWLEDGEMENTS

Milton Mount College closed in July 1960, but the school still lives on in the hearts and minds of its former pupils, most of whom maintain contact through their Old Girls' association – the Miltonian Guild. This is their book.

The factual history of the school has been well documented in three small books: 'Annals of Milton Mount College', by Selina Hadland, Lady Principal from 1873 to 1889; 'The History of Milton Mount College 1871 to 1946', by Hilda Harwood, senior English mistress from 1917 to 1945; and 'The History of Milton Mount College 1946–1962', by Marion L Farrell, Headmistress from 1939 to 1960.

In 2015 the Committee members of the Miltonian Guild realised that the Guild's members were getting old – none was born later than 1950 – and their number was growing fewer, yet there was still a wealth of memories in their minds that needed recording before it was too late. An appeal for these memories resulted in an avalanche of material, which has now been examined, sorted and compiled into a book which is surely unique. It is not possible to acknowledge all individual contributions – we would surely leave some out – so here is an enormous collective "thank you".

Special thanks must go to the three histories mentioned above and also to the booklet 'Cream Horns and Handstands' by Pat Palmer, published in 2012, which has provided a large amount of material. Thanks are due, too, to the West Sussex Record Office at Chichester, who meticulously maintain our archives and have provided many of the photos for this book.

PREFACE

In 1920 Milton Mount College moved from its original site in Gravesend to Worth Park, which had been the home of the Montefiore family since the 1850s. The history of the school's time at Worth Park is well documented, but what has been missing until now has been a record of what it was actually like to be a pupil at the school in the magnificent setting of the mansion and park.

This book plugs the gap and is a remarkable achievement in its own right. It is not the work of one author who interviewed some of the former pupils, but a truly collaborative effort, with personal memories from many contributors synthesised into the final informative and entertaining volume by a dedicated and talented writing and publication team of Miltonians. That this is possible more than 50 years after the closure of the school at Worth Park in 1960 is thanks to the Miltonian Guild, the association of its Old Girls which still flourishes today.

The Guild currently holds an annual reunion (usually at Worth Park) and once a year publishes a remarkable magazine to keep its far-flung members in touch. These are the people who were at school at Worth Park while Milton Mount College was there. Through the Guild network, memories have been collected from all over the country and indeed abroad. The book comes alive with photos from the archives as well as personal quotations which comment on the house and park and aspects of school life and are reproduced in italics throughout the book. The book also reveals something of the personality and enduring friendships of the contributors and the lasting influence upon them of their time at school. Miltonians are a remarkable breed, as witnessed by the longevity of the Guild and its members. Since first becoming acquainted in 1983 with former pupils of Milton Mount College, I have often heard it said that "There is something special about Miltonians". Yes, indeed there is!

The school having closed and so no new generations coming along to take over, the Guild too will eventually cease to exist. This book will stand as a memorial to its members and is a unique contribution to the history of Worth Park.

Margaret Abraham
Former Principal of Wentworth Milton Mount

August 2016.

MILTON MOUNT COLLEGE FROM THE AIR

1598

CONTENTS

SETTING THE SCENE

When Milton Mount College came to Worth Park, in West Sussex, in October 1920 the school had already been in existence for nearly 50 years.

The Rev William Guest, minister of Prince's Street Congregational Church in Gravesend, wanted to found a school in England on the same lines as a female seminary in the USA for the daughters of Congregational ministers. Back in 1864, it was shown that out of hundreds of free endowed schools for middle-class education, almost all excluded girls, although one in seven women at that time were supporting themselves by professional work and thus needed to achieve a high degree of literacy. Few Congregational ministers could afford high school fees, and widows of ministers were in an even worse financial situation.

It was becoming evident that up to 30,000 teachers would soon be needed in British elementary schools, so the College was set up not merely as a school but as a training centre for teachers.

A site was chosen on a hill in the village of Milton, near Gravesend (hence the name), and the Foundation Stone was laid on 5th October 1871 for a school to take 150 pupils. The school opened on 16th May 1873 and remained at Gravesend until 1915. Finance was always a problem, and in 1902 it was decided to admit – as well as ministers' daughters – other girls whose fees would not be subsidised.

Following a bombing raid on Gravesend in June 1915, it was necessary to find a safer home for the school, and accommodation at the Royal Agricultural College at Cirencester was rented until the summer of 1920, when the Agricultural College was fully reopened.

After the war a return to the buildings at Gravesend proved undesirable. The buildings had been used both as a hostel for munition workers and as a naval hospital where patients with venereal diseases were treated. Some members of staff would have resigned rather than return. The search began for a new home in pleasant surroundings.

Thanks to several generous loans, it proved possible to purchase Worth Park mansion, the home of Sir Francis Montefiore, with about 80 acres of land at a cost of 30,000 guineas (£31,500 – equivalent to £1.5 million in 2016). After some basic alterations, the school opened to pupils on 21st October 1920. The official opening ceremony was performed on 23rd June 1921 by Dame Margaret Lloyd George, wife of the Prime Minister, David Lloyd George.

Meanwhile the school governors pursued a claim against the Admiralty for £73,000 (in relation to the Gravesend buildings) but it was not until 1924 that the Compensation Court awarded the school a sum of £35,350 with costs.

Headmistresses at Worth Park:

Miss Anne Askew WOODALL, MA	To 1926
Mrs Dorothy Margaret HENMAN, MA	1926–1939
Miss Marion Louise FARRELL, MA	1939–1960

Miss Woodall oversaw the construction of the music rooms in 1923 and also plans for a three-storey extension to the left of the main entrance. This consisted of a dining hall, above it a dormitory for junior girls, and above that an art studio. Opening day in 1926 was postponed due to the untimely death of Miss Woodall. In her will Miss Woodall left a sum of £500 (equivalent to £27,000 in

2016) towards the cost of a gymnasium, and the Cadbury family offered to bear the rest of the cost. The Anne Askew Woodall Gymnasium (now Milton Mount Community Centre) was formally opened on 27th October 1927 by Mrs George Cadbury, Miss Woodall's sister. The Miltonian Guild (which had been set up in 1888) provided £200 for the equipment.

Miss Woodall was succeeded by Mrs Henman, a widow with a son and a ward. It was decided to build a separate house in the grounds so that she would have a proper home for her family. This still exists, but is now two flats. Mrs Henman was instrumental in providing well-equipped science and domestic science rooms in the quadrangle (the former stables) and also a swimming pool which opened in 1935.

Headmistress's house

Mrs Henman resigned in 1939 due to poor health and Miss Farrell began her duties in August 1939 when war was imminent. Life con-

3

tinued more or less as normal, apart from gas mask drill and air raid practices, until June 1940 when the school was commandeered by the War Office in order to accommodate Canadian troops. Many famous Canadian regiments were based in Sussex between 1940 and 1944. The school was given one week in which to evacuate the building. The only available 'removal men' were about 100 Canadian soldiers – but first the girls had to be removed! Miss Farrell had to trawl the country for suitable premises and eventually the Imperial Hotel at Lynton in North Devon was chosen.

On 7th June 1945 came the news that Worth Park had at last been derequisitioned, but the damage done to it by the Canadians was so extensive that there was no possibility of the school returning for the autumn term. It was not until 1st May 1946 that the school reassembled at Worth Park. The grounds were in a sorry state with army huts dotted about, the tennis courts and games field ruined, and flower beds a mass of weeds. Nevertheless Miss Farrell wrote of "a joy unspeakable to be coming home so we can begin the constructive work of restoring the School to what it was".

Tributes to the Headmistresses:

Miss Woodall: *"Few Headmistresses have had so many difficulties and crises as fell to her. The terrible strain of the early days of the War; the air raids and uprooting from Gravesend; the inconvenience of Cirencester; the finding of a new home...any one of these was enough to make the time of her administration memorable in the annals of the school."* (Miss Condor, her predecessor)

Mrs Henman: *"The School and Guild have lost a wise and forceful leader and a generous and sympathetic friend. Her memory will be treasured by Miltonians everywhere."* (Miss Farrell, her successor)

Miss Farrell: *"We trusted her wisdom, we respected her judgement and we enjoyed her company. She had a lively, sparkling mind. Her vision and her ability to communicate was perhaps her greatest gift to us. The Sunday services at which she preached were ones we all looked forward to... She put before us standards of thoughts and behaviour which became part of us."* (A former pupil)

This aerial photograph, taken looking straight down to the ground, is thought to have been shot in the summer of 1946 or 1947. It clearly shows the round pond and the ha-ha, together with the school buildings and the swimming pool. The area to the north of the swimming pool has evidently been cultivated quite extensively.

Unexpectedly, the lake is almost completely empty. The sun is casting the shadows of the trees very clearly, and any open water, such as that in the swimming pool, appears black, but the whole lake bed is visible. It is likely that the lake was drained during the war, since the stream that feeds it flows up to what was then RAF Gatwick and it may have been feared that the Luftwaffe would mount a Dambusters-style raid in retaliation.

Photograph reproduced by kind permission of Brightmaster Ltd, whose website showing this and many other air photos can be found at http://ukaerialphotos.com

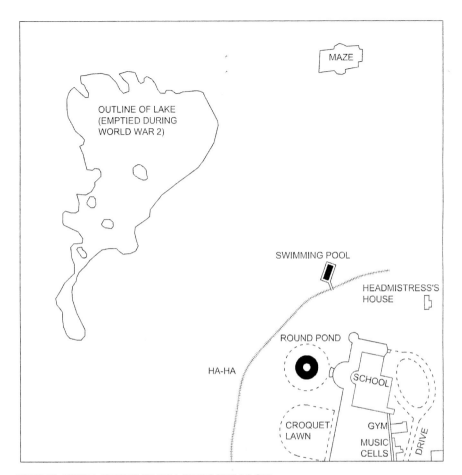

MAZE

OUTLINE OF LAKE
(EMPTIED DURING
WORLD WAR 2)

SWIMMING POOL

HEADMISTRESS'S
HOUSE

ROUND POND

HA-HA

SCHOOL

CROQUET
LAWN

GYM

MUSIC
CELLS

DRIVE

KEY TO AERIAL PHOTOGRAPH (OPPOSITE PAGE)

The outlines of the most prominent features of the Milton Mount grounds are shown above, to the same scale as the photograph, in order to make it easier to identify them

The ha-ha itself shows up very nicely, owing to the shadow cast into it by the mid--morning sun. and the round pond and swimming pool are also easily seen. The main school building can be seen, although its outline is broken up by shadows from the various changes in the roofline, etc.

The straight section of the camellia walk is just visible, together with the gym and the music cells, but probably the most obvious other feature is what is marked as the "croquet lawn". This is what it has become again now as part of , although of course in Milton Mount days it was used for tennis courts

The maze (right at the top of the photo) appears totally overgrown, presumably because little was done to maintain it during the war.

7

THE GROUNDS

The gardens in which Milton Mount College was situated once formed part of Worth Forest, an ancient woodland and hunting ground dating back to Anglo Saxon times, and a medieval farmhouse stood on the site for many years.

We were privileged to be surrounded at Milton Mount College by what, in later years, was to become a landscape of national and local importance, as this circular tour of the grounds will show.

The long drive

Pupils accessed the gardens by the mile-long driveway (now Milton Mount Avenue) which had once been the Montefiores' direct route to Three Bridges station. It was bordered by sweet chestnut and pale green lime trees which flowered in June and gave a strong aromatic scent. Behind these on either side were the remnants of an ancient wood with wild flowers and plenty of wildlife, massive redwoods with doormat-like bark, and rhododendron thickets, the last two planted in Victorian times. If you know where to look you can explore the foundations of the glass houses and nursery beds of the former Victorian kitchen gardens, where a philadelphus tree grew. The top of the drive led to the carriage drive, a circular lawn with big cedar trees in the middle, which took you to the front entrance of the building. We, however, had to enter via the tradesmen's entrance to the left!

The east front before the 1926 extension

After the extension was complete

To the far left of the building (as seen from the drive) was a long, curved camellia walk with a wooden shingle roof, patterned tiled floor and huge glass panels, held in place by ornate oak frames on the outer section, and with camellias growing up the entire length of the inner wall. We were only allowed access to the part of the camellia walk nearest the school in order to enter the music practice cells which were located behind the camellia walk.

The camellia walk in its heyday

In front of this was the formal garden, which was out of bounds as it was the staff garden. Known as the Dutch garden, it included the lawn, a fountain and a sundial garden, which had short, clipped hedges and seasonal planting, not dissimilar to a parterre layout, bordered with Pulhamite edging.

The celebrated family of James Pulham & Sons was involved in the creation of picturesque rock gardens, grottos, water features and ferneries which were fashionable in the Victorian and Edwardian periods. When natural stone was not available, or was prohibitively expensive, heaps of rubble were coated with cement and the surface modelled to simulate the texture and colour of natural stone. This proprietary material became known as Pulhamite. The Pulham family also manufactured a range of ornamental garden ware including urns, vases, balustrades and sundials, sometimes in terracotta but also in Pulhamite.

The Dutch garden in the 1920s

Down a slope from here was a vast lawn with some of the numerous specimen trees which grew on the estate. This was ideal for our outdoor plays as there were two natural levels, the higher one being used for the stage, and the lower one for the audience.

Further down still was terracing, balustrades, pillars and urns designed by James Pulham. Beneath these structures were the grass tennis courts (now returned to the original purpose as a croquet lawn), a small summer house – the footprint of which can still be seen – the hard tennis/netball court and the "Village Green" where the Brownies and Guides used to meet, overshadowed by a huge lime tree which was great for climbing. This is now called the Star Garden.

The round pond, 1926

Moving round to the back of the building to the upper Italian terrace and down the steps you found the round pond with its fountain basin and lily pad containers, all made of Pulhamite. It was encircled by 'plum pudding' yew tree topiary. The fountain in the middle was working for the opening ceremony in 1921, but no Miltonian alive now has any recollection of it being functional after that. When the contractors drained the pond for refurbishment they found a layer of mud three feet deep. No doubt this was because we always washed our muddy wellies in the round pond!

The fountain was restored to working order in 2016 although the lily pad containers were not reinstated. One of them was in the possession of the family of Fred Dench, a former gardener. The family returned it when the gardens were being restored and it is now located near the Star Garden and contains seasonal bedding plants. We spent a lot of our free time in this area and played hide-and-seek in the nearby mauve rhododendron bushes. The scent of the yellow and orange azaleas is a potent memory for many Old Girls. Both the pond basin and the fountain are now Grade II listed.

In this area too were many specimen trees including a tulip tree, a mulberry, a ginkgo and a monkey puzzle and many of these are still there. The rarity of these was impressed upon us. Occasionally girls would be asked to pick flowers for a special event such as Concert Day but it was stressed to pick only rhododendrons, not azaleas – because they grow comparatively slowly.

The uninterrupted vista ahead was across parkland, the ha-ha, fields and an ornamental lake. The walled ditches known as ha-has were – and still are – a common feature in country estates from the 18th century and were intended to be invisible from the house while keeping cattle from straying into the formal gardens. But in our day the ha-ha kept us in, as beyond it was out of bounds!

The lake (marked as a fish pond on a 1932 map) was Alpine in character with two substantial Pulhamite islands, and a third (recently afforded Grade II listing) in the form of a rock outcrop with a bonsai yew tree growing on it. On three sides there was formal planting of trees and flowering shrubs. However, there were occasions

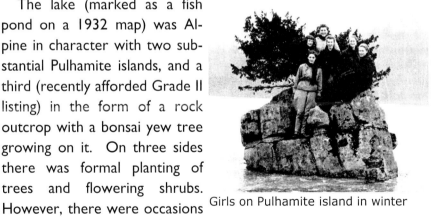

Girls on Pulhamite island in winter

when there was official access to it. For example, if the lake froze and there was a sufficient thickness of ice for skating on it, or when supervised 'wet walks' took place around it. It was inevitably visited at numerous other times! It was also a source of frogs and small pond life for biology studies.

Girls on rabbit gate, 1950s

At the right hand end of the ha-ha, as viewed from the school, was a rabbit fence with what we knew as the 'rabbit gate', through which we reached the swimming pool. The wire rabbit fence was installed to exclude rabbits from the formal gardens. In 1953 after the outbreak of myxomatosis it kept any diseased rabbits away from the school and out of our sight. Each evening two senior girls were required to check that the rabbit gates were properly closed. Periodically we would see the gardener sneaking out at dusk, gun under his arm, but we did not ask questions.

Now the outdoor swimming pool, diving board and changing hut came into view. The water had to reach 60°F (16°C) before we were allowed in, and then only in the summer term, when it was in use every day apart from Sunday. Continuing in this direction one accessed the games field where lacrosse was played in winter and cricket and rounders in the summer. The field was out of bounds if not taking part in sports lessons or match fixtures. Even further beyond the games field was the maze in a rougher area containing many birch trees, hawthorns, brambles, wild flowers including orchids, and wild strawberries. This area was definitely out of bounds, although it was often used by the Guides for tracking and camp fire making.

Girls gardening

Heading back past the swimming pool, at one time there were small gardens here, tended by those pupils interested in growing things, and Nissen huts left by the Canadians after the Second World War.

The big surprise in this location, however, is the large Pulhamite fern rockery, the existence of which was unknown to any of us until after the school closed as it was in the Headmistress's garden – a place where we did not go! The rockery also is now Grade II listed.

Further along on the left is the entrance to the quadrangle (known by us as the Quad; now called Ridley's Court), on either side of which two white magnolia bushes thrived. These were passed every day by the boarders housed there and also pupils attending science or domestic science lessons in the rooms round the courtyard. Now back at the top of the drive, the circular tour of the grounds is completed.

Pulhamite rockery in 2014, cleared for replanting

Apart from the summer house, games field, maze, swimming pool, pupils' gardens and Nissen huts, and of course the mansion itself, most of what has been described remains in situ. However the Montefiores would not have seen their planting mature as we did, and the grounds are not exactly as we left them. They are a living thing and will go on evolving, being loved and appreciated by the new residents and by Miltonians looking back with fond memories of their time spent there.

The quadrangle or "Quad". The clock was removed when it became unsafe

...*going to bed one night to the sound of heavy rain, waking up to a wonderland. The frost had come while everything was dripping – every branch, twig and green thing was coated in a sheet of ice, decorated with icicles and beads of frost. We were taken down to the maze by a member of staff to see just how beautiful it was. (1947)*

Approaching the frozen lake, 1954

The Dutch lawn in snow, 1954

Plum puddings with custard!

THE BUILDINGS

Worth Park mansion was built in the 1850s for Sir Joseph Mayer Montefiore. It had ten entertaining rooms, a billiard room, ten principal bedrooms with dressing rooms, four bathrooms and numerous smaller rooms for the servants. The stable block or quadrangle (renamed Ridley's Court) has a date of 1881 and these buildings are now Grade II listed. The estate was inherited by Sir Francis Abraham Montefiore (1860–1935), the son of Sir Joseph. He moved to Farmleigh on Grattons Drive in 1915 and put the estate up for sale. Crawley Library has a copy of the sale catalogue; the estate was estimated to cover 2,055 acres. Milton Mount College bought the mansion and surrounding gardens (80 acres) in 1920. Apart from the war years (1940–1946) the school remained there until it closed in 1960. The mansion was demolished in 1968 and a block of flats built in its place.

ENTRANCE HALL AND READING ROOM.

The saloon (left) and atrium

The house had been built in grand style with fine details and the chief rooms were magnificent. The walls of three of them were covered in gold silk brocade although this was beginning to fray by the 1950s and the lower parts were covered over with plywood. The imposing main entrance gave on to an atrium with painted ornamentation.

The main corridor looking towards the Dutch garden

The main corridor, which went from one end of the house to the other, was wide with polished parquet flooring and two fine marble fireplaces. The principal rooms contained huge mirrors in gilded frames above the fireplaces. These mirrors, we were told, had been covered by boards during the War in order to keep them intact after one drunken Canadian soldier had fired at his own mirrored image!

The main corridor looking towards the atrium. The school's honours boards are visible on either side. The school bell can be seen near the fireplace.

Ceilings on the ground floor were high, also embellished with mouldings and gilding. The main staircase which rose from the entrance hall had a banister supported by decorative ironwork depicting musical instruments. A small piece of this was 'acquired' by an Old Girl just before the building was demolished. The thick doors were mostly of mahogany, and some had panels of elaborate etched glass.

The upper floors were less grand although the principal bedrooms, which became large dormitories, also contained ornate mirrors and fireplaces. Unfortunately the fires were never lit for us and we learnt to endure unheated bedrooms.

Memories are hazy about the lighting. One girl was impressed in the 1920s with "electric light in every room", but another memory of that era recalls "sewing by gaslight" (perhaps in the Quad).

The staircase, first landing

Fragment of ironwork

The Assembly Hall. This was on the south west corner and had originally been the billiard room. It had gold silk brocade on the walls and ornate carving. Morning and evening assemblies and two Sunday services were held here accompanied by a pianist on the grand piano. The windows were huge and at the right time of year there were wonderful sunsets during evening assembly.

The assembly hall. The grand piano was just out of the picture to the right

Singing and music theory lessons were held in this room, as well as external music exams. The room was also used for night time fire practices. The whole school with their red or grey fire blankets off their beds had to make their way to the assembly hall by the quickest route; this often meant using a staircase which was normally out of bounds.

The saloon

The Saloon. This was to the right of the main entrance and was a general common room. It was used for dancing on Saturday evenings and other hobbies during the week.

Room S. This was on the south side looking towards the Dutch garden and was exclusively the common room for the 6th forms (Years 12 and 13).

It contained a large fireplace and comfortable chairs. Its finest feature was a tondo (a circular work of art) in the ceiling painted with the sky and several small birds – quite an eyesight test to count them all. There was a picture of the Doge of Venice in his green robe and high hat. We had a wireless (radio) in there and we listened to 'Grand Hotel' and other popular programmes. We also used gramophones belonging to some of the girls and spent part of our pocket money on records. Guy Mitchell was popular in the 1950s – "She wears red feathers…" and "Sparrow in the treetops…"

Room S

The Chapel. This was a small room on the top floor opened in 1950. The chairs were donated by some Old Girls and anyone could use the room for prayer and quiet contemplation. Mrs Walker always put a vase of flowers there, as she did in the assembly hall.

The Library. Originally built as a winter garden, it was first the dining room (1920–1926) but then became the library. It had a mosaic floor and a distinctive glass dome, which can be clearly seen in all the postcards and photographs taken from the round pond.

The library, 1926. Plants from the former Winter Garden are still visible

Sadly the dome leaked and there was a selection of orange bowls and buckets in strategic places to catch the drips! However on a sunny day it was a lovely light room in which to sit, sink into one of the ancient wicker chairs, and get lost in a book. Books were often donated by Old Girls and there was a catalogue of the stock. Girls had to sign to borrow a book and hopefully at the end of term all books had been returned. A daily newspaper was provided.

The Science Laboratory. The school had pioneered the teaching of science to girls as long ago as 1883. At Worth Park a dedicated laboratory was located in the Quad which housed all the necessary equipment.

Science lab in the late 1950s

The Domestic Science Room. This was also in the Quad with plenty of cookers, table space and treadle- and hand-operated sewing machines. The 5th and 6th forms could use the room after summer public exams. Some girls had not cooked or made clothes in school because they had followed an academic curriculum. These two rooms were apparently sited away from the main school building because of the possibility of the girls starting a fire!

The Theatre. This was in the basement and contained a table tennis table. It was also used for lectures and films as it was large enough to accommodate the whole school. It had no natural light and there was a small raised area as a stage complete with sash windows through which dramatic and sometimes disastrous entrances and exits took place. There was a cine projector and also an epidiascope – a huge contraption which took two people to lift, and which projected pictures on to a screen by pulling a lever.

A cookery class, 1939

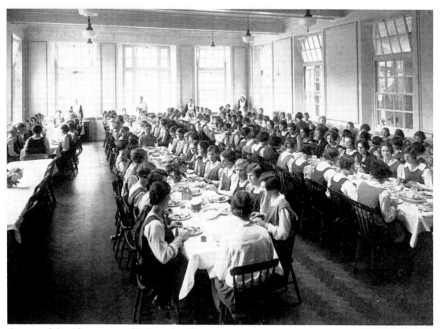

A meal in the new dining hall

The Dining Hall. Added in 1926, it became a multi-purpose room. The tables, which comprised long planks joined side by side and resting on metal trestles, could be removed for such events as Speech Day and Concert Day. They could also be turned over showing the bare wood instead of the black painted upper side.

> *I recall their being used for writing exams or sometimes homework, and any tedium could be relieved by poking out the stale crumbs from the joins between the planks.*

The Art Studio. This room occupied the top floor of the 1926 extension, its many windows providing the best possible light. A raised area at one end allowed models (inanimate or live) to be staged for drawing lessons. In the 1920s some talented girls in the school's art club painted a series of panels in watercolour, intended as a studio frieze, showing stylised aspects of school life. These were exhibited at the Royal Drawing Society in 1923 and 1924.

The art studio pre 1940, showing part of the frieze

The Artesian Well. An artesian well is a well in which water rises under pressure from a permeable stratum overlain by impermeable rock. So did we have one and did it need a pump as one Old Girl recollects?

> I remember asking an older girl what the intermittent clanking noise was. She told me this was the pump of an artesian well, which drew up water from beneath the building. I can't imagine that the well supplied all the water for a building housing 200+ people! Possibly it just supplemented the mains supply – or perhaps it was used for watering the gardens? Is the well still there?

INFORMATION TO PARENTS

Girls were admitted after their eighth birthday and not as a rule after the age of 15, following completion of an entrance examination. They were not usually allowed to remain after the end of the school year during which they reached the age of 18.

There were up to 200 boarders and about 20 day girls in the school each year. The annual fees for boarders in the 1930s were 125 guineas (£131.25, equivalent to about £8,000 in 2016) plus additional charges for use of school books and stationery, medical oversight and laundry expenses. Extra fees were charged for optional subjects such as music or elocution lessons and horse riding.

Girls could take scholarship examinations between the ages of 12 and 15. There were a junior and a senior scholarship and two Halley Stewart scholarships for the Congregational ministers' daughters. The successful candidates had the appropriate sum deducted from the accounts sent to parents. The honours board in the main corridor featured the names of all previous winners.

Rules (from the 1940s and 1950s). These included:

- Girls are expected to return on the day when the school re-opens, unless they are prevented by illness.

    My sister and I had special permission to return a day late in January 1949 as we had been invited to the Lord Mayor of London's party at the Mansion House.

- There is no holiday at half term or Bank Holidays. Girls may not go away from school during the term except in the case of serious illness at home or the wedding of a brother or sister.

- A medical examination by a doctor must take place every January and the signed form sent to the Headmistress three days before the school opens for the spring term.

- Pocket money is paid to the house mistress at the beginning of the term and dispensed weekly and every girl keeps her own accounts. Parents are asked to inform the house mistress in writing what amount, not exceeding 1/- (one shilling, now 5p) is to be handed out weekly. Chief expenditure is Sunday collections, stamps and stationery.

  Our house mistress, Miss Davey, was the maths mistress so our account books were meticulously inspected. Any error, deliberate or otherwise, had to be corrected before she would hand out our money for the week. To this day I keep my financial records in good order.

- No jewellery except a brooch or watch may be brought to school and no girl is allowed to have scent, face powder or cosmetics of any kind.

- Only the following shampoos may be used: Vaseline, Silvikrin, Gloria and Wrights Coal Tar.

- No eatables, except sweets, jam and spreads, fresh fruit and birthday cakes, may be brought or sent to school. Cakes will be shared as they cannot be kept.

- All letters sent out of school are supervised, except those to parents or near relations.

- No girl may receive (or make) telephone calls. If the matter is urgent the call should be addressed to the Headmistress who will decide what can be done.

  In the 6th form I had the chance to buy some material to make a blouse but needed to know quickly if my parents would pay for it. I wrote home and must have made an impression about an urgent reply. I received a telegram: "Certainly buy material. Writing. Mother." A telegram would have been delivered by a man or boy on a bicycle and create quite a stir. I expect the Head herself opened it to make sure it was not bad news.

- Girls may go out with visitors on Saturdays only provided that those visitors are known to the Headmistress or that written permission has been received from home. They are free after 1.15 p.m. on Saturday and may be out for the whole afternoon and evening. They may go out on Sunday after the morning service, but must return for the evening service which takes place at 5.45 p.m. No girl may go out more than three times in the term.

We had Saturday school in the mornings and if you were due to go out you couldn't leave until after lunch. My brother, who was in the Army, had a racy little red MG sports car and I gained much kudos by his occasional arrival to collect me, while the 6th form hung out of their window by the front door gazing in wonder at his handsome visage.

Cycling group, 1954

Senior girls were allowed to bring bicycles to school and could go out on Saturday afternoons in groups of five – remember we had no telephones. If an accident occurred two girls could go for help and two stay with the injured one.

School Reports. Each term a report was given to us to take home to our parents. Obviously it had comments from each subject teacher with exam results, if applicable. The Headmistress wrote under General Remarks. It also gave the number in the form and the average age of the form.

We were weighed and measured at the beginning and end of term and the figures were entered in the report.

In 1947 I was 4ft.9½ins. and weighed 5st..9lbs.

When I left in July 1955 I was 5ft.5½ins. and weighed 9st.7½lbs.

One girl's inventory from the 1950s

Uniforms. Uniforms had to be bought from Daniel Neal & Sons of Kensington High Street, London, or C.G. Southcott Co. Partnership of Leeds. We had a trunk each which the railway would collect and deliver in advance (PLA – Passenger Luggage in Advance). Lorries would deliver these from Three Bridges station to the luggage entrance near the kitchens. On the first day of term they would be brought upstairs in the dumb waiter to the bedrooms. We would unpack them and lay everything out on our bed, in the order of the inventory, each item folded so that the name tape showed.

Every single item, including detachable collars and hankies, had to have a name tape. This was all checked by the house mistress before putting away. The packing/unpacking process was an impressive event, carried out with military precision, and we became skilled at it – a skill most useful in later life.

Lacrosse team in gym tunics, 1933

Uniforms changed from decade to decade, gradually getting more up-to-date, although the ubiquitous dark green tunic was a constant. The original style was round-necked and A-line with a fixed waist but, later, there was a different style, pleated from the yoke and a girdle worn around the waist. This happily accommodated any size or shape of girl!

In the 1920s a tussore silk blouse was worn underneath with a green and red striped tie (tussore, or shantung, was a coarser and cheaper silk from the tussore moth rather than the silkworm). At some stage the tie was discontinued, apparently because the Sister (nurse) at the time decreed it was 'unhealthy' – although it was later reinstated.

> *There were very long black (wool) stockings and black knickers so we were always neat and tidy when we did gymnastics.*

In the 1940s the green tunics were still the same – four inches above the knee when kneeling – but the silk blouse was replaced by Viyella for the winter, and the black stockings replaced by knee-length socks held up with garters and brown lisle (smooth cotton) stockings for the senior girls. There were also liberty bodices, a thick bodice with rubber buttons worn in addition to a vest for ex-tra warmth. These also had buttons at the bottom to which sus-penders could be attached if necessary. We wore two pairs of knickers – white cotton underneath and thick green ones (green bags), which had a pocket for a hankie, over them. In the summer we discarded the green ones with great relief except for gym les-sons. They tended to make you bulge.

On Sundays we had dark green repp (fabric with a ribbed surface) dresses with white detachable collars so they could be washed. They fixed with press studs (poppers) which often got mangled by the laundry so that they didn't fasten and scratched one's neck.

In the summer we had grey linen divided skirts, quite short, and short-sleeved Aertex blouses, plus striped cotton dresses with

Summer dress

Summer uniform

yellow, blue or green stripes and Peter Pan collars for evenings. The Sunday version had different green stripes which we called music stripes.

In the early 1950s senior girls were allowed to wear grey flannel skirts instead of tunics. They had to be no more than five inches below the knee. They were very popular, being much warmer and more flattering than tunics.

We also had green cardigans, blazers with a school badge on the pocket and mackintoshes with a detachable hood. There were green wool winter coats but these became optional on account of expense. Hats were originally black velour for winter and panama for summer, but later changed to grey felt with a green band for all seasons. Overalls had to be worn for science and domestic science lessons. Swimming costumes were made of a thick black material which took ages to dry.

Winter coats and macs, 1950s

The list of footwear was impressive – outdoor shoes, indoor shoes (low heels and straps), games shoes, gym shoes, wellingtons, galoshes and bedroom slippers. Sandals were permitted in the summer but not to be used on a regular basis. We had separate socks for games which had to be marked with a green wool X on the ankle to identify them. They did not get washed too often!

Mrs Walker organised a second-hand uniform shop. This was helpful to parents struggling to keep up with the huge number of items required, especially if their daughter grew rapidly.

THE STRUCTURE OF THE SCHOOL

Any school has to have a structure, but for a boarding school this has to be especially strong, as the school is in effect a home for its pupils for more than half the year. Each of the three terms was about twelve weeks long, with no half term break. To compensate for this we had an eight week holiday in the summer, and four weeks each at Christmas and Easter.

Milton Mount was essentially a boarding school, but parents living within easy reach of Worth Park were able to send their daughters as day girls. The full complement in September 1947 was 168 boarders and 22 day girls, a fairly typical distribution of numbers. Day girls received exactly the same education as their boarding counterparts, including afternoon games and Saturday morning lessons, and were encouraged to participate in evening and leisure events as far as practicable. They were also allocated to a house to add to the sense of belonging.

Saturday morning school was demanding – it seemed to mess up weekends. There was always homework to sort out, leaving little time to relax.

I remember one girl from Copthorne who occasionally came to school on her cob horse, which she tied up near the pet sheds – quite a novelty to all.

The school also welcomed a number of girls from overseas. They may have been British girls whose parents lived and worked overseas, girls whose parents wanted them to have a British education, or occasionally girls whose parents had fled from unstable countries.

In all cases it was essential for them to have a British guardian to whom they went in the holidays if they were not able to go home to their parents.

Exams. Every girl had to pass an entrance test before being accepted by the school. During the course of each term there were monthly subject tests and the Headmistress would keep a close eye on the results. At the end of the year we had subject exams, in classrooms, and the results were on our end-of-term reports. External exams were taken in the art studio or sometimes the dining hall. Language oral exams took place in the Headmistress's house.

The School Captain. This was democratically decided. Towards the end of the summer term the Headmistress would nominate three girls as possible candidates for the forthcoming year. An election was then held, every girl casting her vote. In this way the girls had their choice, but the Headmistress ensured that the chosen girl was suitable for the role.

Privileges. Sixth formers were automatically given certain privileges, such as having their own bicycle at school. It was also possible for those in the Upper 5th form (Year 11) to be awarded a privilege badge, if the Headmistress considered a girl suitably responsible. One of her favourite sayings was "privilege goes with responsibility".

An early privilege badge

The School Parliament. The school had its own parliament, which was set up in the 1930s and met once a term. Representatives were elected from the houses and from the forms, and proposals for discussion were submitted to the School Captain a few days before Parliament was to meet. The staff attended and took part in debates; they could not vote but had the power of veto, which they used chiefly when the motions passed could not reasonably be implemented. Debates were often lively, and on the whole the girls took them seriously and sensibly. The discussions also improved communication between staff and pupils.

Topics ranged from the sensible to the trivial, such as:

• Reinstatement of the school magazine in 1947;
• Society meetings to be held in the late afternoons so that day girls could participate;
• Revision of the disorder mark system;
• Provision of badges for games captains;
• Shorter girdles for the junior school;
• Setting up a fund for fireworks for Guy Fawkes celebrations;
• Formation of a committee to decide on suitable radio (and latterly television) programmes for the school;
• Numerous discussions about the Eisteddfod, which was finally abolished in 1955.

The Houses. From 1927, Milton Mount was divided, structurally as well as socially, into houses. Previously, as at Gravesend, these had been called corridors, and took their name from the member of staff in charge of them, but the layout of the Worth Park premises rendered this arrangement less practical. Each house was to be named after a famous pioneer in exploration or social work; the chosen names were put on slips of paper in a bowl and in the presence of the whole school each corridor mistress drew a name. Thus, Miss Marsden's corridor became Shackleton House, named after the Antarctic explorer; Miss Mathew's, Scott – again after a polar explorer; Miss Harwood's, Raleigh (after the Elizabethan adventurer); Miss Batson's, Gordon (after the general); Miss Luce's, Livingstone (after an African explorer this time); and Miss Cockburn's, Havelock (named after Sir Henry Havelock, a British general who served in India and died at the Siege of Lucknow). Havelock House was dissolved in 1933 and its girls distributed among the other houses. The youngest pupils lived together in

Shaftesbury House (named after Anthony Ashley Cooper, 7th Earl of Shaftesbury, who was a noted social reformer and president of the Ragged School Union).

It is interesting to note that all these were men. The first house mistress of Shaftesbury was Miss F L Eldridge, so her initials were FLE and her girls quickly became known as The Fleas.

Some Fleas in 1947

Apart from Livingstone House, which occupied part of the Quad, each house was allocated to a segment of the building, and girls were not normally permitted to go into another house. A senior mistress looked after each house, assisted by another mistress, each having their own single bedroom. The girls slept in dormitories holding between two and ten people. Each house had a prefect and vice prefect who shared a bedroom for two, often with a fireplace which could be lit on Sundays and toast and cocoa made! The larger dormitories then had a prefect who supervised the girls.

A comfortable 'two room', with a saucepan of milk on the fire

Each girl had a strip of coloured ribbon sewn on the left yoke of her gym tunic; blue for Scott, red for Shackleton, yellow for Livingstone, salmon pink for Gordon, and pale green for Raleigh. House loyalty was very strong, as was rivalry in sporting events, tidiness, deportment and drama. At the end of each term, cups were awarded to the house achieving (a) the best tidiness (our drawers were inspected without warning!), (b) the fewest disorder marks – which were given out by the staff for a range of misdemeanours, and (c) good deportment.

Starting in the late 1940s, each senior house had a record book, which was maintained by the house prefects. Only that for Raleigh House survives; it gives annual lists of girls in their house by form, the senior and junior sports teams, and a summary of the year's achievements or failures. In some instances, former pupils' further education or significant events are noted.

Shaftesbury House was, of course, a bit different. Girls aged eight to ten needed a bit of 'mothering' and this was provided for many years by Mrs Walker (nicknamed Ma Trotter) who was Shaftesbury house mistress as well as school matron. Being a mother herself she had great empathy with the younger girls and was much loved by them. The house had its own mascot, a doll called Jemima Porter. This is a report in the Miltonian of 1926 by Form IIIb (Year 5).

"In the Autumn Term (1925) we had Jemima Porter's birthday party, which is held on November 9th every year for the lowest form. We all brought our dolls and animals of all descriptions. Miss Woodall and Miss Eldridge were the hostesses..........

We began by playing Hunt the Thimble. Then we went to the Saloon for tea and, while we were having it, the new Jemima Porter, who is a little doll, was passed round. She was wearing a school cap, a blazer and a blouse and skirt. There was a lovely cake in memory of the old Jemima Porter, who was left at Gravesend."

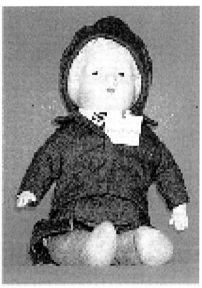

Jemima Porter

Later, the party was held in the Headmistress's house. And some years later, when the school merged with Wentworth College in Bournemouth, Jemima moved to the renamed Wentworth Milton Mount and assumed their dark blue uniform.

The dormitories. Dormitories were far from luxurious. In the early years at Worth Park, the rooms had curtains and each girl had a cubicle separated from the others by a cloth screen. After the return from Lynton there were no cubicles and no curtains. The floors were of bare wood, roughly varnished to guard against splinters.

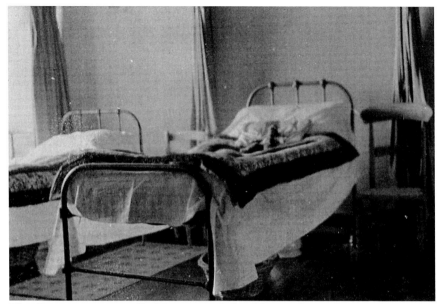

The Dungeon, so called because it had barred windows. This prevented girls from climbing out on to a ledge. Taken in the 1920s or 30s, when each girl in the dormitory had a separate cubicle

The hanging arrangements comprised a long rail with a curtain; other clothing and personal items were kept in large chests of drawers – usually one shared by two girls. Shoes were kept in a large oval wicker basket beneath each bed. Once a week there would be a shout of "Beds Up" which meant that you had to place the basket on your bed and turn up the overhanging blankets so that the maids could easily sweep underneath. The beds were basic – iron frames with horizontally arranged wire springs. These were mostly saggy and often had protruding bits of wire. From 1947, each girl had to provide her own sheets, pillowcases, towels and serviettes – the Ministry of Education would not allow the school to purchase new sheets. Blankets were provided, and each girl had a fire blanket, in rough red or grey wool, which she was expected to wrap round herself in the event of night-time evacuation in case of fire. An eiderdown or extra blanket could be brought from home. Mattresses were turned frequently which involved the chore of stripping the whole bed. It was obligatory to use 'hospital corners' for tucking in the sheets.

Bathrooms and toilets. Each house had its own bathroom with baths and wash basins divided by canvas curtains for privacy. Toilets were in separate

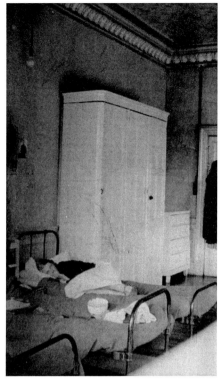

A big dormitory

rooms. At Gravesend the dormitories were long corridors with toilet facilities at the end. The euphemism "Please may I go to the end of the corridor?" quickly turned into "Please may I go tend?" and this phrase stuck forever afterwards.

At Worth Park the toilet block on the ground floor was a separate, unheated, building accessed through a draughty covered way. No temptation to linger. Those in the basement were even worse with tiny windows and very high ceilings. It was like sitting in a dark chimney.

Baths had a line painted at a certain level to indicate the amount of water allowed. We had a rota of baths three times a week. Hair washing, however, was scheduled once every three weeks unless a request for more frequent washing was received from parents.

Electric fan hair driers were fixed to the wall and these were often turned on just to warm up the room!

The laundry system. The house colour system had another function. Each garment had to be 'blobbed', i.e. a small square of coloured embroidery silk had to be sewn on to it next to the name tape (by the reluctant pupil), so that laundered items could be returned to the correct house.

Every week each girl was expected to place her dirty washing into the appropriate heap on the long back corridor. We tended to hold our breath when passing by the piles of dirty clothes! These were then put into large wicker hampers and taken downstairs in the dumb waiter for transport to the laundry at Horley. The clean laundry would be returned to the individual houses to be reclaimed.

View from a top floor dormitory

THE SCHOOL DAY

Mondays to Fridays

Our life was ruled by bells.

In the main corridor was a large hand bell. This was rung at 6:55 am (first bell) and then again at 7:20 am (second bell). If you were still in bed after second bell the house prefect would come and make sure you got up. We were required to assemble at 7:45 am in an orderly line ready to go down to breakfast, led by the house mistress who would make a note of anyone who was late.

At 'High Table' in the dining room there was a smaller hand bell. Talking was not allowed until the mistress in charge of the meal rang the bell. Equally when the bell rang at the end of the meal, talking stopped.

Tower Bell…..

This was an impressive bell high up in the building with a long rope. It was used when we were out in the grounds or playing games. Senior girls were allowed to ring this bell on occasion. It required a good deal of effort and skill.

Although the school day began with the bell at 6:55 am, at that time of day most of us just muttered "first bell", turned over and went back to sleep. However, a few of us had an early music practice, so had to get up, dress and go down to the music cells. In summer this was no problem. In winter the cells were very cold and it was not fun. Other pupils who supposedly had flat feet had to get up and go down to the gymnasium for exercise on their feet. Again – no fun in winter.

But, as a general rule, everyone had to get up by the time the second bell had rung at 7:20 am, dash down to the wash room, dash back to get dressed and be ready to line up outside the house mistress's room to be taken down to breakfast. Those who were late received a disorder mark. To ensure orderly progress to breakfast, the girls were lined up in pairs, starting with the youngest, and led downstairs or across from the Quad by their house mistress.

I remember the strident call of Miss Davis, in charge of Gordon on the first floor landing, to Miss Lunt, her Raleigh counterpart on the second floor: "Are you coming down Marjorie?"

In the 1920s the teacher in charge of breakfast used to read to the girls from the daily newspaper. In the 1950s a radio was installed in the dining room and the bell was rung for silence just before 8 o'clock so that we could hear the news. Just before the news headlines there was often an SOS message from someone who had lost contact with a friend or relative and wanted to know if anyone knew where they were. No Twitter or Facebook in those days!

Post was distributed at breakfast and my sister always opened the letters from home first and I had to keep asking her to let me see them.

On a weekday, we went back upstairs after breakfast to make our beds and tidy our rooms before making our way to our form rooms for registration, and then to the assembly hall for morning prayers and any daily notices. All the staff assembled at the front, facing the girls, with the youngest girls sitting nearest to them and the senior girls at the back. One of the music teachers sat at the grand piano ready to play the hymn. At that point the School Captain went to tell the Headmistress that the school was ready. We could always hear her coming since the stairs from her office were right next to the assembly hall. And in she would come, gown flowing, and of course all the girls stood up when she arrived. We were also expected to stand up when our teacher entered the form room and greet her by name.   The girl sitting nearest the door was expected to warn the others when the teacher was approaching.

Most people use ballpoint pens these days, but although these were invented by the Hungarian Laszlo Biro in 1938, they were not widely available in the UK until the 1950s. So we had to use either pens or 'dip pens' with a replaceable nib fitted into a wooden handle. We therefore had inkwells which required regular replenishment by the form's ink monitor. The ink was kept in a chilly room near the kitchens, which doubled as the flower room.

Our forms were quite small (usually 25 maximum, sometimes less). One year a form exceeded the specific size and had to be divided into two, with separate form teachers. This must have caused problems for both staff and accommodation.

The morning was taken up with the usual lessons with a short break at 11:00 am when we had a drink and a very stodgy bun (if we wanted!). After lunch there were two further lessons before everyone had to take part in some kind of exercise. This was usually games – in winter netball and lacrosse, in summer tennis, rounders, cricket and, when it was warm enough, swimming. Every pupil was supposed to swim as often as possible. This could be in gym lessons, during the afternoon games period or in our leisure time in the evening when we would be supervised by a member of staff. If it was raining, wet walks were organised, usually by the house prefects. In any case during that hour we had to be outside in the fresh air whatever the weather.

For the younger girls the timetable differed as they had their games time before lunch. After lunch they went for a rest on their beds before having three more lessons in the afternoon.

TIMETABLE FOR IIIA, Autumn Term 1949
Average age: 10 years 10 months.   Number in Form: 20.

	Monday	Tuesday	Wednesday	Thursday	Friday	Saturday
1	Arithmetic	Art	Arithmetic	English	Arithmetic	Arithmetic
2	Singing	Art	Scripture	History	Gym	History
			BREAK			
3	Geography	Study	Art	Dancing	Geography	
4		Gym	Art	English	Study	
5	GAMES	GAMES	GAMES	GAMES	Nature Walk	
			LUNCH			
6	Study	English	Study	Arithmetic	Nature	
7	French	Music	Grammar	English	Needlework	
8	Rhythmics	Study	Scripture	French		

Name of mistress by teaching subject:
Form Mistress: Miss M. D. Turner; Arithmetic: Miss B. George;
Geography: Miss B. George; French: Miss M. Lester Lewis;
Art: Miss J.P. Allen; Gym: Miss M.D. Turner; English: Miss J.P. Allen;
Music: Miss H.M. Parry-Davies, Miss F.M. Lee; Scripture: Miss Farrell;
History: Miss H.B. Kohn; Nature Study: Miss J.P. Allen;
Needlework: Miss J.P. Allen; Dancing: Miss M.D. Turner.

Then it was time for a quick wash and change into our evening clothes. We only wore our blouses and gym slips (or, in the summer, divided skirts) during the day, and had to change into dark green dresses or cotton dresses four nights a week. On Wednesday, Saturday and Sunday we could change into what we called non-uniform. Then we went down in our houses for tea followed by evening prayers. The hymns for evening prayers were always chosen by us at the beginning of each term. Every class had to submit a list of about 10 favourite hymns from which the Headmistress would choose the one for each evening. Sometimes we got the list back if our choices were, according to the Headmistress, a bit unimaginative. Certain hymns made regular appearances with "The day Thou gavest, Lord, has ended" being a particular favourite.

After prayers we went back to our form rooms for 'study'. This was our homework period usually supervised by a prefect. The juniors only had to do about 30 or 40 minutes-worth before being free. As we progressed up the school, study could last almost until bedtime, especially if we were working towards exams. But Miss Farrell was obsessive about us having a period of time between work and sleep, so she would often check that we were not working for at least half an hour before bed.

Relaxing in the library....

However, there was quite a bit of leisure activity in the evenings. There was a Brownie pack and a Guide company. There were various societies run by ourselves. The library was available for anyone to use and many of us would go down to the music cells to play for fun instead of doing set practice. There was also an orchestra. In the summer we would go outside to explore, play tennis and generally enjoy ourselves.

Relaxing on the terrace

In the winter we might stay in the classroom and listen to records played on some lucky pupil's wind-up gramophone. Juniors could go down to the basement and play in the theatre – a large room with a low kind of stage and an extremely old piano with some keys missing. Seniors could go to the saloon and listen to pop music on Radio Luxembourg.

Bedtime varied, with the juniors going upstairs about 7:45 pm, middle school about 8:45 pm and the seniors about 9:15 pm. Once our house mistress had checked that we were where we were supposed to be and that we had read our bit of scripture assigned for that evening, the school was silent from about 9:00 pm. Those of us who came to bed later did so without a word.

We could read our own books, of course, before going to sleep. I read all of the "Jennings" series and annoyed the dormitory prefects very much by my giggling during the silent period. I even used to read under the bedclothes after I was supposed to be going to sleep!

Saturdays. These were of course different. We still had a couple of lessons in the morning and then it was back into form rooms for about an hour to sort and (if necessary) mend our clean laundry. This was then inspected by, usually, the house mistress. Those of us who were senior enough to wear lisle (pre-nylon thick cotton) stockings often had to darn them because they used to get caught on chairs and desks that had splinters.

Who now remembers darning holes with wooden mushrooms? My mushroom was a neat affair whose top unscrewed and I kept darning needles inside. I still have it.

Those of us with a set of clothes in good repair would produce these same items for inspection each week to avoid having to mend the others.

Those of us who were lucky enough to have a visitor (usually a parent) to take us out for the afternoon presented ourselves at the staff room to ask permission to go. A member of staff would have a signed permission slip from Miss Farrell's secretary to indicate that we were allowed out. Then it was out until bedtime.

The rest of us had all sorts of different things going on. There may have been matches against another school for those of us who were athletic. About once a month on a Saturday afternoon a walk to Crawley was organised for girls to go shopping. Known as the Crawley Crawl, it was quite a hike (4 miles round trip) but we were not allowed to use the local buses.

If you were a sixth former with a bike you might go out with a group of friends to a local beauty spot. In the summer you would almost certainly be outside somewhere – the grounds were the most marvellous place in which to play. After tea there might be a film in the theatre, a concert in the dining hall or we might just entertain ourselves with dancing or listening to music.

Russian dancing on the terrace, February 1955

LESSONS AT MMC

As in today's schools, there were a number of subject choices. English and Maths were, of course, compulsory up to O Level, Maths being expanded into arithmetic, geometry, algebra, logarithms and trigonometry as you progressed up the school. In the 6th form there was the option of Pure and Applied Maths. English was divided into Language and Literature, as these were the O level subject titles.

Some subjects, such as History and Geography, could be dropped in favour of something else such as German or extra Art or Music lessons. In the Lower 6th there was the option to study Civics (citizenship and government) to O level standard.

French lessons began in the Upper 3rd (Year 6) and Latin in Middle 4th (Year 8). Very often modern languages were taught by a French (Mamzelle) or German national. Latin up to O level was essential for those planning to apply for certain university courses.

All the sciences were taught by Miss Foster (who acquired the nickname "Fizzy"). She had to cope with biology, botany, chemistry and physics. Physics was not her strength, but she was excellent at biology and botany. In fact she could often be seen tending the gardens around the Dutch garden on Saturday afternoons; she also kept bees. Later she received help from some visiting part-time teachers.

I remember watching frogs mating in the fish tank in the library and being quite enthralled. Miss Foster patiently explained what was happening.

Art, Domestic Science and Music were choices which could be made by less academic girls. Art lessons included the usual drawing and painting as well as crafts such as papier mâché, basket-making and lino-cutting. Domestic Science included fairly basic cooking skills, as well as dressmaking, embroidery, smocking and appliqué.

We learnt useful things like how to make pastry by not getting the flour on the palms of your hands, only the fingertips. I still make excellent pastry!

Religious Education. We had church membership classes, sometimes led by Rev Clifford Hall who was for many years Chairman of the Board of Management, sometimes by Rev Norman Garnett (a pupil's father) from Christ Church, Pound Hill, and sometimes by Miss Farrell. Then those of us who were non-conformists were received into church membership at a Sunday morning service. For Church of England girls, confirmation classes were arranged with the rector at Worth.

Our regular religious education was taught entirely by Miss Farrell. She took every class once a week for RE, and her maps of the Middle East – always drawn on the blackboard with great sweeps of chalk – were famous. She had an unusual view of some things, though. She used to tell us that The Devil must have been really attractive, otherwise he would have had no influence. Our RE was basically Bible study and no other faiths were mentioned. At bedtime we had our Bibles at our bedside and we were expected to read a passage every night.

Careers Advice. Academically clever girls were of course encouraged into university education, though very few attained Oxbridge places. Some of them studied medicine or similar. For the less academic, Miss Farrell outlined their career choices in a magazine article.

They will hope for a career of use in the community, which offers interesting work with expectation of reasonably good remuneration

and security. If it proves to be one which can, if necessary, be con-
tinued after marriage, or will be a good preparation for wifehood and
motherhood, so much the better. Length and cost of training will
also have to be considered.

The three main spheres she mentioned were domestic science, nursing and work among children. This last presumably included teaching. She also suggested work in "the great stores" or secretarial work, or for those achieving sufficient GCE passes, librarianship. For those girls wishing to work out of doors or to take up journalism, she outlined the various drawbacks.

Sex Education. This was extremely elementary. The Lower 6th form members were ushered discreetly into Room S for a short talk by a female doctor. In fact it was merely a biology lesson about the reproductive system with pictures and what to expect during pregnancy. That was it.

SUNDAYS AT BOARDING SCHOOL

Since the school was originally a religious foundation (as many schools were in the 19th century) and was set up to provide education for the daughters of Congregational ministers so that they could provide for themselves when they left school, Sunday was a day for religious observance.

However, after breakfast letters had to be written to parents. Every girl had to bring a writing case to school each term with paper, envelopes and enough stamps to last the term. We often wrote to other people as well – our brothers who may have been at Caterham School, friends and other relatives. The only problem here was that our house mistress could read these letters before they could be sealed and sent. So many girls found other ways of posting these letters. Day girls were very useful.

Then, those who were Church of England sometimes went up to Worth Church for Sunday service there.

Once a month the Church of England girls walked to Worth Church which was about one and a half miles from the school. On one occasion we were taking up the first two rows. I was leading the crocodile so I went to the far end of the first row and we were in full view of the choir. The morning service was well under way and we were singing the words of the psalm 'Come let us kneel and fall down unto the Lord our God' when the floorboards gave way underneath my feet and I landed on top of the heating pipes. The choir boys were ecstatic. I had difficulty climbing up again because we were very tightly packed in the front row and it took some time for the other girls to move up and then lift me out. I had managed to tear my lisle stockings and graze my leg in the process. The Church has been rebuilt since, after a fire caused by an electrical fault, and has been modernised with new floorboards and pews.

The rest of us had a service in our beautiful assembly hall. This was often taken by a Congregational minister. Sometimes he came from Fen Place (now the Alexander House Hotel in Turners Hill) which was a retirement home for Congregational ministers and their wives.

One retired minister came regularly to preach. He was quite doddery and his sermons were punctuated with "Er....er....." To relieve the boredom, one girl decided to try and count the number of Ers and this soon became a game. Then it was decided it would be easier to turn over a page of the hymn book each time and lots of other girls joined in. The result was a frequent loud swish of paper amid stifled giggles. Looking back it seems a very unkind thing to do. I wonder if he realised what we were doing.

Sometimes the father of one of us took the service and then came to high table afterwards for lunch. His daughter was then able to sit beside him. We enjoyed that. If no minister was available, Miss Farrell took the service. The singing was always good. Our choir was well trained and often performed choral pieces for the congregation.

....the joyful singing of hymns and the choir's lovely anthems. Recently at our church we had "Lead me, Lord", and at once I was transported to MMC with an uplifted heart.

At the end of the 1950s, when a Congregational Church was built just beyond the bottom of our school drive, we would walk down there three times a term for morning service and sit together in the gallery.

Sunday being a day of rest, we all rested after lunch. In winter it was a silent rest on our beds. We used to read, sew, knit and, when the sugar ration was lifted after the war, eat sweets. In summer we were allowed out in the grounds (what is now Worth Park Gardens) and there was more freedom. We could venture as far as the maze unseen and look for wild strawberries.

However, after tea (with the post-war rationing making it not the most exciting of meals – perhaps Spam and a piece of lettuce, but we did have cake!) evening service was for everyone. If the minister who had preached that morning had stayed on, he took the service. If not, Miss Farrell was again in charge. She was an excellent story-teller and would often take as her subject the story of one of our heroes after whom the school houses were named – Shaftesbury, Livingstone, Shackleton, Scott, Raleigh, Gordon. To this day we still wonder why all the heroes were men! Sometimes, however, she would tell us the story of a heroine, such as Florence Nightingale, Edith Cavell or Elizabeth Fry. We loved these sessions. Following the evening service our form mistress would read to us from a book of her choice, after which the rest of the evening was free.

Some choices were more exciting than others. When the book was Jamaica Inn we could hardly wait for the next episode. We were wise to the fact that she left out a few pages, but we were able to take a sneaky look afterwards and catch up on the naughty bits.

On the last Sunday of the summer term Miss Farrell had a special sermon for those girls who were leaving school. We called this The Big Bad World and it was the same each year. Basically it was a warning about all the pitfalls and temptations we would encounter. It was not taken too seriously!

Sundays were mostly quiet days – too quiet for those more energetic amongst us. But they had a calm and routine feeling about them which many of us appreciated.

SPORT

A 1930s school prospectus stated that "girls are encouraged to take part in the various games – lacrosse and netball in the winter and tennis, cricket, rounders and swimming in the summer. Also there is a large and well-equipped gymnasium and girls have regular gymnastics lessons". It was most unusual in those days for a girls' school to play cricket. In fact the parents of twin daughters chose MMC for their girls for that very reason. Games were compulsory Monday to Friday afternoons except in bad weather, when there were 'wet walks'. The local children would watch us walking in crocodile formation and referred to us as the 'greengages'. If you could claim a legitimate health problem you might be excused games, but still had to go for a walk.

As well as matches against other schools there were very keen inter-house matches each term. The winning house was rewarded with a cup.

In Livingstone we have memories of 7:00 am match practices when the house matches were imminent. It was not popular on an icy, cold and frosty winter's morning to have a netball or lacrosse practice before breakfast!

Other schools played against included St Michael's Limpsfield, Roedean, Rosemead, and Trevelyan. And each term we challenged the Old Girls. We regularly took part in the annual lacrosse tournament at Merton Abbey in South London.

The schedule of games was posted on the notice board in the main corridor opposite the library with details of what each girl was doing.

There was a long corridor in the basement where outdoor shoes and socks were stored as well as mackintoshes. We also kept our lacrosse sticks and tennis racquets there. We will never forget the smell of foul socks and the linseed oil which we used to oil the lacrosse sticks, and Miss Turner telling us to oil our guts! Lacrosse was played on the large games field beyond the swimming pool and netball on a hard court (constructed in 1930) near the Village Green.

Lacrosse circa 1950

I remember being terrified as a goalie in lacrosse games – all those galumphing girls rushing towards me with lax sticks raised on high. Help!

The outdoor unheated swimming pool was opened in 1935 after seven years of fund raising. Parents, governors and Old Girls made contributions, large and small, and the girls raised money by putting on concerts and plays, making sweets and handicrafts for sale. The

Photographic Society sold prints of school photos at 2d each, the domestic science department did laundry work, and the Guides attended to the parking of cars at various local events. Most notable of all efforts, however, was that of Rev A G Sleep (Secretary to the Board of Governors) who, during a voyage to America aboard the 'Celtic', dived into the ship's swimming pool with all his clothes on, thus raising the magnificent sum of £50 (the equivalent of more than £3,000 in 2016).

The pool had a large elevated water inlet (visible above left) at the shallow end and at the deep end it originally had a three-tier diving board, followed in 1949 by a springboard (see above right). To swim out of one's depth it was necessary to achieve the Deep End Pass; swim two widths, jump in and tread water, and do elementary life saving over a single width. We were not allowed in the pool until the water reached 60°F (16°C) and we would watch the maintenance man put his thermometer in the water hoping it was warm enough.

The summer house

There were five grass tennis courts (now once more a croquet lawn) and a small summer house, originally the Garden House presented to Miss Marsden and Miss Keeble on their retirement to their house in Horley in 1934. Miss Keeble gave it to the school in 1947. Look carefully now and you can see the concrete base on which it sat on the north side of the croquet lawn.

Tennis courts, 1920s

Each summer Mrs Janet Brenchley gave a tennis racquet to the winner of the under-16s singles tournament. Her daughter Mary subsequently married the steeplechase jockey and author Dick Francis.

The Anne Askew Woodall gymnasium (now the Milton Mount Community Centre) was opened in 1927. The facilities were excellent with wall bars, ropes, a pommel horse and a box.

We were taught to climb, vault and do some exotic moves like 'longfly handspring' over the box, for which two strong girls were required to catch you in case of mishap. Less strenuous exercises helped our balance and the younger girls had a weekly session of rhythmics. This was basically dancing (or prancing) to music played by one of the music teachers whose style of playing was rather staccato, ideal for rhythmics. In the 1930s a girl wrote about the exercises:

Knees bend, arms up, stretch.... Also deportment when we marched around the room to music singing "Head up... Shoulders back...."

The gym in the 1930s

Not all girls enjoyed sports, however.

I managed to avoid sports and gym mostly by being involved in music – piano, viola and school orchestra – which successfully got me out of two games sessions each week. In the gym I usually sat on the springboard to avoid having to jump or climb.

The springboard was the jumping-off platform for the box and horse which was anchored by a girl sitting on each side.

My dread was gym. The pommel horse was really awful. I was hopeless.

Cricket in the 1930s. Later, divided skirts were worn for games in summer

My school report for games and swimming was monotonous – Very fair! However in the Lower 6th – Margaret has shown herself to be a most useful and efficient cricket scorer.

At one time we had inter-house sports competitions, with athletics events and various less formal ones like the sack race shown below.

Sack race, 1932

MUSIC AND DRAMA

Music. Milton Mount had an excellent music department from the beginning, with at least four music teachers and sometimes more. From 1893 pupils were regularly entered for the Royal College and Royal Academy of Music examinations and a number distinguished themselves, including Jessie Marsden who later became a music teacher at MMC, and Joan Davis who became a concert pianist, being examined for her LRAM by Ralph Vaughan Williams. Her parents donated the Bluthner grand piano for the assembly hall. It was used for piano exams and was a real treat to play.

At Worth Park, after 1923, music lessons were held in the music cells, which were approached from the camellia walk. The music mistresses had rooms with decent windows but the practice rooms were a series of small, dark cells. Each cell had a small window in the door so that you could be observed – no chance of getting up to any mischief. Soundproofing was minimal with a resultant cacophony of sounds.

View from the music cells to the main building

Girls who showed talent on the piano were encouraged to take up another instrument: usually violin, viola or cello. Thus a string orchestra was formed, although it was made up of girls at very different levels of ability which limited its range somewhat. However a performance of Haydn's Toy Symphony with added percussion was very successful and Handel's Firework Music was also popular.

One of the music mistresses, Miss Arnold, also gave lessons on the recorder and started a Recorder Group. Sometimes they joined the orchestra for special events. (Miss Arnold, later Mrs Barnett, subsequently taught music at Wentworth Milton Mount).

Those who became proficient at the piano were expected to play for evening prayers and for Sunday evening services. Playing for evening prayers involved learning just one hymn, but Sunday services required a suitable piece at the beginning and at the end. No problem with the end, but the beginning was tricky. The pianist would have to be able to bring the piece to a quick ending with some clever improvisation as soon as the Headmistress walked in – nerve-wracking.

After the return from Lynton, each May a Concert Day was held to which parents and friends were invited. Sometimes this would be a series of solos, duets and some orchestral pieces. Some years a whole production was performed, such as 'Il Trovatore', 'Dido and Aeneas', 'Hiawatha's Wedding Feast', and 'Merrie England'.

When Miss Marsden retired as senior music mistress in 1933, she was succeeded by Miss Winifred Kent. Nicknamed 'The Duchess' (shortened to 'Duche') she commanded respect. Always immaculate in high heels, twin-set and pearls, with well-coiffed hair, she was, quite simply, terrifying and no girl would dare misbehave in her classes.

Not only was she an excellent music teacher, but her many productions of operas and concerts were of an extraordinarily high standard. In addition she was a fine and creative needlewoman. For

'Dido and Aeneas' in 1949 she made muslin dresses for the six little girls in the cast, together with sashes and headbands covered in exquisite, hand-made, paper flowers.

Il Trovatore, 1947

In 1954 she excelled herself with a performance of 'Merrie England' by Edward German. She had been able to manage most of her productions with female voices only, but 'Merrie England' required tenor, baritone and bass voices. It was with great pride that she announced to the school "I have produced three men". Not a titter nor even a smile.

> *During my first term in Shaftesbury House, I opened a door believing it to be my dormitory, to find a warm, luxurious room, lined with long swathes of beige satin curtains, perfumed with Turkish cigarette smoke. I felt I had fallen into a dream. A large lady then rose up in the midst, an ivory cigarette holder in a hand heavy with cabochon emeralds…..saying: "Wrong room! Wrong room". The lady, I was told, was Miss Kent.*

Learning the piano was optional and an additional cost to parents. However the whole school had to participate in singing lessons. We were made to repeat a line time and time again until Miss Kent was satisfied. Woe betide any girl who omitted a final 'T'. 'Silent Night' was particularly challenging. However there could be lighter moments. One girl recalls singing 'Four and Twenty Blackbirds' to the tune of the Hallelujah Chorus. Good singers were allowed to join the school choir, which performed on special occasions and would often add a descant to one of the Sunday hymns.

Drama. Being on two levels, the Dutch lawn was ideal for outdoor productions, and senior girls would usually put on a play during the summer term. In the winter, plays could be performed on the stage in the dining hall.

Alice in Wonderland, 1930

Some girls were able to have elocution lessons. This was not about having posh accents, but more to do with oral delivery, projecting the voice, enunciating clearly and focusing on the audience.

Sword dance, 1932

The Winter's Tale, 1952

In 1941, while at Lynton, an inter-house Eisteddfod was intro-
duced, initially to raise money for Barnardo's. This got bigger and
bigger, eventually with competitions in music, drama, verse speaking,
needlework, painting, crafts, and country dancing. Every girl was
expected to enter at least one category, especially as one mark was
awarded just for entering! However, more and more time was being spent on this and eventually, in 1955, it was abolished by the
School Parliament.

The Boy with a Cart, by Christopher Fry, 1955. Produced by Miss Lunt (seated centre)

A Midsummer Night's Dream, 1958

SPECIAL DAYS

Speech Day. This took place each November and became a military operation! Girls who were to receive awards were systematically lined up in their houses and then walked round the school, finally going down the staff staircase near Miss Farrell's study. The staff, all wearing their gowns, had to make sure the girls were in the right order. Girls who had left school the previous July and were returning to receive awards had their names on the appropriate chairs. Prizes were always books, chosen by the staff, and as the certificates for external exams never arrived on time they were usually represented by blank sheets of paper. We were told not to forget to polish the backs of our shoes as this is what the audience would see.

The guest speaker – or his wife if applicable – presented the awards, and a parent proposed a vote of thanks seconded by the School Captain.

Visitors' Days. The first report of a Visitors' Day is in July 1947, when there were displays of dancing, tennis and swimming for the families of the girls. In later years there were drama presentations including 'The Boy with a Cart' and excerpts from 'The Merry Wives of Windsor', 'The Winter's Tale', the operetta 'Barbarina', 'A Midsummer Night's Dream', and 'Much Ado about Nothing'.

One year there was a mannequin parade showing clothes made and modelled by senior girls, which was followed by 'A Mozart Musical Evening' performed in the dining hall. Miss Lunt (Head of English) wrote the dialogue which conveyed the mannerisms and conversation of people living in 1785. Miss Lee worked very hard in supervising the music, which included piano, violin, cello and clarinet solos and some charming singing.

In 1952 the Guides, Brownies and Rangers showed various aspects of Guiding. To end the display they all assembled around a camp fire to sing. A catastrophe alas! The asbestos on which the camp fire was burning exploded and would have caused confusion among those gathered around had not the Guides truly lived up to their motto – Be Prepared.

Old Girls' Days. Once a term Old Girls were invited to school for a day when we challenged them in the various sports. The Dramatic Society would often perform a play on these occasions.

Royal Occasions. During the first few months of 1937 the thoughts of the Empire and all patriotic Miltonians were centred on the Coronation. Only a few of us were able to see the actual procession, but we all managed to celebrate the occasion. Those who went up to London saw everything: even those who – not having seats – stood in the crowd. Having seen the decorations in the capital, they returned to find the school no less patriotically bedecked; in their absence the main corridor, saloon and dining hall had been adorned with flags, bunting and tri-coloured streamers. For the first time the school visited the Horley cinema to see the film of the Coronation procession and in the evening there was hilarious singing round a bonfire skilfully constructed by Callaby, the gardener.

May 6th 1947. A half day holiday in honour of Their Majesties' Silver Wedding.

January 25th 1949. Visit to Crawley by HRH Princess Elizabeth. The school attended the service of dedication of the New Town and the ceremony of naming a road (Manor Royal) in the industrial area. Her Royal Highness passed the school gates in the afternoon and, to our great delight, waved to us as we lined the route.

Pupils chatting with the Queen Mother

July 8th 1952. *One particularly memorable occasion was the day a group of us were allowed to cycle over to the opening of a new home for retired ministers at Fen Place a few miles away. It was to be opened by the Queen Mother.*

What excitement! The Headmistress gathered us together to learn how to curtsey and how to address the Queen Mother in the unlikely event of her noticing us. We were not to say 'Your Majesty' but 'Ma'am'. When we arrived, we joined the crowd assembled on the front lawn to watch Her Majesty plant a tree. We stood in a cluster as close as possible. The hole had been prepared in advance and she was handed a small silver trowel.

As she straightened up, to much applause, her eye was caught by the group of green-clad girls and she walked right up to us and spoke to us. "Hello girls, where are you from?" "Oh, we're from

Milton Mount College" we replied in chorus. "How far away is that?" Again we replied in chorus, all beaming with delight, and completely forgetting our morning's coaching. We were thrilled by this encounter with royalty and with the photograph in the national press the next day.

May 30th – June 3rd 1953. Coronation Holiday

The majority of the school went home. Some were fortunate to see the procession from stands or windows on the route; others braving the elements on one of the coldest nights in June slept on the pavement, wrapped in coats and rugs. What stories there were to tell when everyone came back to school! For many it was the first time they had watched television. Those fortunate enough to have one invited many friends and neighbours to squeeze into their front rooms and watch on their 7 inch black and white TV! Later, it was possible to go to one of the inexpensive news theatres (small cinemas) and watch it all in colour. These news theatres were very popular and a way of keeping up-to-date with international news stories when television was in its infancy.

On the Sunday after the Coronation those senior girls whose parents lived abroad were privileged to attend the Commonwealth Youth Service in Westminster Abbey, at which the sermon was given by the Archbishop of Canterbury, Geoffrey Fisher.

June 9th 1958. We were honoured in being asked to make a presentation on behalf of Crawley Secondary Schools to Her Majesty, Queen Elizabeth, when she visited Crawley New Town. The gift was a workbox for Princess Anne which was made by the Upper 5th Domestic Science class under Miss Appleby's supervision. It was covered in royal blue silk embroidered with the Sussex Martlets (mythical small birds) in silver thread. It was presented by the School Captain together with an anthology of Sussex, hand lettered and illustrated by the girls of Notre Dame School. In the morning Miss Farrell had been presented to the

Queen at the College of Further Education in Crawley. In the evening we saw, on television, the Queen planting a tree in Queen's Square.

Girls who slept in the Quad were annoyed by Miss Appleby working late into the night on the workbox and keeping them awake with the noise of the old treadle machine.

May 6th 1960. Whole day holiday to celebrate Princess Margaret's wedding to Antony Armstrong-Jones (later 1st Earl of Snowdon) and the boarders were allowed to watch the ceremony on the school's black and white TV.

EXTRA-CURRICULAR ACTIVITIES

At Worth Park, every girl had an hour each evening to use as she pleased. Possiblities were many – Dramatic, Literary and Musical Societies flourished, as did the Dancing and Badminton Clubs and a small Art Club. The school also had branches of the Council for Education in World Citizenship (CEWC) and the Student Christian Movement in Schools. The formal Dramatic Society usually produced a play to be performed at Old Girls' Day in March, but some enthusiasts wrote and performed their own plays, often without a script.

Home-made shows were encouraged and usually the Lower 6th (Year 12) who were not involved in external exams would put on a play or revue. Some witty songs were written and fantastic costumes made. Parents were persuaded to donate such things as bowler hats and old bedspreads which could be cut up for dresses.

About once a term a film would be shown, such as 'Great Expectations', 'Moby Dick', 'The Small Miracle', 'Three Smart Girls', 'Whisky Galore' and 'Genevieve'. There was the inevitable hiatus while the projectionist (the science mistress) changed the reel and sometimes the film broke and had to be repaired speedily. Much hilarity resulted when the film 'Harvey' could only be shown at half speed.

Around 1950 one girl, whose parents were much involved with the rehabilitation of prisoners (and keeping them off the drink), founded a branch of the Guild of Abstaining Youth. Membership was denied to any girl who had imbibed alcohol, and the club, known as the GAYs (well before the name took on its modern meaning), became a closed affair, holding meetings convened in dark corners and arranging social events accompanied by soft drinks.

Lectures from outside speakers were regularly held, with such varied topics as UNESCO, Vitamins from Crookes Laboratories, Penal Reform, Wild Animals as Pets, Town & Country Planning (by Col. Turner of Crawley New Town Development Corporation) and Travelling with a Circus by Brian Vesey-Fitzgerald.

On one notable occasion, the CEWC welcomed a prominent politician of the day, David Ennals MP, to present a lecture and then dine with the members. Girls were asked to dress in national costume of any country belonging to the United Nations Association; one participant remembers dressing as an Egyptian with baggy trousers, fez or tarboosh, and a curved wooden dagger!

We were honoured to have visits from prominent musicians, including the London Orpheus Choir, the Bristol String Quartet, Leon Goossens, the Chelsea Singers and Yehudi Menuhin. Small groups were also taken to the Dr Ernest Read concert at the new Festival Hall in London, 'Madame Butterfly' at Sadler's Wells, and 'Swan Lake' at Covent Garden.

Outdoor Activities. One legacy of the Army's occupation of Worth Park was a pair of Nissen huts which had been decorated with questionable drawings by the Canadian soldiers. One of these became the pet shed, in which girls could keep rabbits, mice or guinea pigs. The other was used for a time to store gardening tools, and latterly became garaging for staff members' motor cars.

I had mice! If I see a mouse now I am pleased to get on to a chair to avoid it, but I had mice in the pet shed as did other friends. On the 3:48 train from London to Three Bridges, we raced our mice in the corridor on the way back to school. One girl in my form tested one of her mice for swimming ability by dropping him from the top diving board. We all thought this was cruel but Hector survived and faced another day.

Girls who wished could cultivate a small patch of land. Others could play tennis in the summer, run round the games field or just walk around the beautiful grounds.

The hard winters of 1947 and 1954 meant that the lake (normally out of bounds) froze and skating was allowed. Not everyone had skates but we were all allowed on the ice. This was greatly enjoyed by the skaters but not so much fun when one just stood on the ice in the cold!

'My garden'

Girl Guides. The Girl Guide movement was very strong within the school, with a Brownie pack, a Guide company and, for a while, Land Rangers. Thoughts of becoming Air Rangers, with links to Gatwick Airport, were shelved, probably for security reasons.

The Guides and the Brownies met once a week, in the evening. Sometimes the Guides would be able to go for a hike or to a County event at the weekend. We did a lot of marching (possibly because our Guider had been in the Army) and won some competitions. Camping was allowed one weekend a year; this was a welcome release from being in school, although we had to go into school on Sunday for morning service and Sunday lunch!!

Some recollections:

> I joined the Brownies aged eight, when I first went to MMC. I was most upset when I was put in the Kelpies. I dearly wanted to be a Fairy or an Elf, which seemed much more romantic. I certainly enjoyed all the activities and dancing around the toadstool on the Village Green. I 'flew up' to the Guides but soon floundered, being particularly hopeless at knots.

I remember singing 'Kookaburra sits in the old gum tree'.

I recall learning and using the Morse Code and, in particular, crawling on our tummies through the undergrowth by the ruined house on Hollerday Hill (near Lynton) in an attempt to acquire a badge for Tracking.

I enjoyed being a Brownie in Lynton days. "We're the little happy Pixies, Getting others out of fixes", or "We're the little laughing elves, Helping others, not ourselves." Later, at Worth, I joined the Guides. I enjoyed the occasional camps, the campfire songs and the sessions of stalking and tracking. Not the knots. I never got my Second Class (badge) because I didn't manage to complete my useful article. I very laboriously made a song-book and gave it in – but too late.

We had one unforgettable night camping down by the lake. We made inedible dampers (blobs of dough wrapped round a stick and 'toasted' on the camp fire) and spent the night in totally inadequate blanket bags; nearly froze to death.

I joined the Land Rangers; this appealed to me because I knew we were able to camp. One Sunday morning a group of us set off on a hike (after a hearty breakfast cooked over the camp fire). As the week before had been wet, we got rather muddy and must have looked a little bedraggled when we arrived at Worth Church for the morning service. However, the Vicar greeted us as though nothing was amiss.

Six of us, two staff members and four girls, went to Chichester Cathedral for a special service and presenting of colours. I felt so moved to see what a wonderful movement Guiding is – there were hundreds of people there from all over Sussex. I am not quite sure who took the service, but he gave us a lovely sermon which I shall not forget. (1953)

I well remember sleeping outside the tent under the stars – magical.

Lunch at Guide camp, 1930s

Washing up afterwards

On more formal occasions black stockings and hats were worn. The next photo from the 1930s has no explanation.

Guides dressed more formally for an unknown event

Brownies, 1949, round their toadstool

Guide camp, Blacklands, August 1949

Organised Leisure. Hallowe'en and Bonfire Night were celebrated under strict supervision (frequently evaded) and a Christmas party was held at the end of each autumn term. For this, a huge Christmas tree was erected in the dining hall, beautifully decorated, and lit by real candles. The science mistress and an assistant stood by with candle snuffers on long poles, ready to extinguish any candle threatening to set the place alight.

Each summer the Staff Dance was held in the dining hall. The girls dressed in their best non-uniform frocks and each had a programme in which to write her dance partners. Girls were expected to ask members of staff to dance – some staff were more popular than others!

Once a term, after a spell in which discipline had been satisfactory, the Headmistress declared a 'conduct holiday'. This was usually preceded by some clandestine murmuring among the staff and we were summoned to the assembly hall in great anticipation.

The remainder of the day was completely our own and we had considerable freedom to do whatever we liked within the school environs.

I remember spending half the day kneeling on the dusty dormitory floor playing 'jacks', all taken very seriously with an umpire.

Outings. Each girl was allowed to go out with her parents or approved close relative three times a term on a Saturday afternoon or on Sunday after the morning service. Girls without family nearby were frequently taken out by other girls' parents, subject to the formal approval of their parent or guardian. A favourite venue was The George Hotel in Crawley where they served an excellent lunch, but for tea the best was John & Mary's (near the Premier Inn on Balcombe Road). Not only did they serve good and reasonably-priced teas, but they had a musical grandfather clock (a polython) and, for a small coin, the owner would insert a large metal disc punched with holes, which would play a tune.

John & Mary's, 1955

An entire class of girls, or two classes together, might sometimes be taken to watch a county cricket match, an opera or a theatrical performance. Shakespeare was particularly favoured, presumably on account of the English Literature curriculum.

Each spring and summer the entire school went on an outing. In summer the younger ones might go to the seaside, whereas the older girls would visit a city or place of particular interest, such as Canterbury, Hampton Court Palace, the House of Commons or one of the London museums.

Fun on the beach

A favourite outing was to the Ideal Home Exhibition at Olympia in London as there were many free gifts handed out.

We joined the queue for free toothpaste samples several times. We thought that because we were all dressed in uniform they wouldn't recognize us, but eventually they realised and we were banned.

I remember receiving a free sample of cigarettes. Very daringly I smoked one of these in the form room, but then panicked that our next teacher would notice the smell.

Many of the outings were reported in the school magazine 'The Miltonian':

In May 1949 the juniors went to Windsor and Runnymede by special train with children from other schools on a trip organised by British Railways. Each school had a guide who told them the history of the castle. Later they climbed the many steps to the top of the Round Tower, where some hats blew off, which were later retrieved. After leaving the castle they went on the river to Runnymede.

The article does not say that we took off our hats and put them on a curtained shelf at the back, having no idea that the curtains would fly open and our hats went into the river! Were they retrieved? I don't remember.

Festival of Britain. On May 16th 1951 the whole school went up to the South Bank Exhibition in London. Two of the most popular pavilions were 'People of Britain' and 'Land of Britain'. Everyone looked with interest at the story of our beginnings and development and that of our countryside and natural resources, which included everything from live and stuffed animals to a working forge and a coal mine.

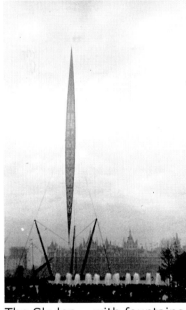

The Skylon – with fountains in front of it

The main attraction was the Dome of Discovery, containing exhibits on the theme of discovery covering the living world, polar regions, the sea, the earth, the atmosphere and outer space. Not many of us managed to get inside as there was a continuous queue, but those who did were most impressed. The solar system and weather reports were too complicated for most of us but we were very interested in such things as prehistoric animals and reptiles and scientific discoveries.

The abiding symbol of the Festival was the Skylon, a futuristic-looking, slender, vertical structure that apparently floated above the ground. The joke of the day was that it was like the British economy, with no visible means of support. If we got lost we were instructed to head for the Skylon and wait there.

(The Dome was demolished in 1952 and its materials sold for scrap. Some of the metal fragments were turned into a series of commemorative paper-knives and artefacts. The Skylon was also demolished. The site was cleared and is now the location of the Jubilee Gardens, near the London Eye).

The greatest difficulty was lack of time, and our progress was further hampered by the fact of having to go round in parties under the escort of the staff, and by the vast crowds. Merely to get a drink we had to queue for over half an hour. However, not even lack of time, a cold wind and a cloudy sky could damp our enjoyment of that day, and we arrived back at school exhausted, but satisfied.

There was a celebration of the Festival at Worth, which included an 'open day' when the public could visit the school.

May 1951

Went to the Festival of Britain with Miss Bell and had a super time. Had a green, white and pink ice and a choc one.

Miss Bell with four of her charges

June 1951

Walked from Hassocks to Lewes via the Downs. It drizzled off and on. Mouldy lunch as was very small. Got famished. Home at 7:50. Had heaps of biscuits.

May 1952

We went to Canterbury; got there at 11:15, back at 7:30. Spent over 2 hrs in the cathedral with a lady guide. Most boring. We all got very hungry. I bought ½lb biscuits.

June 1954

Went to Bosham and Chichester by coach. Quite a nice day. Had a good view of the eclipse. Guide took us round cathedral.

Lower 5th trip to Arundel, June 1954

June 1955

We went to Wisley by coach in the morning and then to Parham. It was a lovely trip despite some showers.

Overseas trips

Foreign holidays and courses for today's schoolgirls have become the norm, but in the 1940s and 1950s they were considered quite an innovation, and were always highly regulated and very firmly linked to some aspect of education.

In the summer holiday of 1951, in connection with the school's membership of the Council for Education in World Citizenship (CEWC, the junior wing of the United Nations Association), several girls in the 5th and 6th forms were taken to Switzerland by two staff members.

We travelled by ferry from Newhaven to Dieppe and then by train to Geneva, changing at the Gare du Nord. We, together with teenagers from other schools, were accommodated in a large and modern Lycée not far from the centre of the city, where we all had morning lectures about the UN. The catering was quite unlike boarding school fare – one day we were even served globe artichokes with plenty of butter. A highlight one day was a visit to the UN headquarters to sit in on a plenary session. Something to do with UNICEF or UNESCO, I think.

In the afternoons we had considerable leisure to explore the environs. We had arrived during Geneva's famed Fête des Fleurs – lots of music, dancing and colourful costumes. Three of us took the cable car up to Salève with a friendly male fellow student who later became a BBC producer! We lounged around on the grass and enjoyed a picnic provided from our lodgings. Subsequently our group travelled to a mountain village, Les Plains sur Bex, to stay in a timber-built lodge under the watchful eye of two ladies: one a headmistress from another school, the other the wife of a UN attaché. Here we went walking in the mountains and had lunch at a mountain hut.

The following year, A-level French students were taken to France by their teacher for some intensive conversational French.

In 1956 a group travelled to Salzburg for the bi-centennial celebrations of Mozart's birth.

It started badly when the ferry from Dover was cancelled due to storms and we had to come back the next day – which meant we had no reserved seats. We found the food in our hotel very bland and unappetising, but attended some wonderful concerts and worshipped in a fabulous Baroque church on the Sunday – not understanding a single word!

FOOD, GLORIOUS FOOD

Ask an Old Miltonian about her most vivid memories of school and near the top of the list would be the food!

Mealtimes were certainly disciplined. Before each meal, girls would assemble in their house corridor, in twos with the youngest at the front, having collected their own serviettes from a basket. It was helpful to have a distinctive serviette ring.

I had a silver serviette ring from India with elephants all round it.

When a gong was rung by a member of the domestic staff, everyone went down to the dining hall in silence. This procedure was properly co-ordinated to avoid traffic jams. At breakfast and tea girls were seated according to their house; at breakfast supervised by the house mistress and her deputy and at tea by the house prefect and her deputy. At lunch seating was in forms, supervised by the form mistress. Staff were given their tea in the Staff Room, which must have been a great relief for them. Sometimes we would see a trolley being taken to the Staff Room filled with an enviable selection of cakes.

Those sitting at high table on the stage, with the Headmistress or her deputy supervising the meal, were selected by rota. All girls would remain standing until grace had been said, then could sit down, but silence maintained until the bell on high table was rung. Then the noise was deafening with up to 200 girls all talking at once.

We all had to take a turn in sitting next to the member of staff at the end of our table and were expected to make conversation.

Some were much easier to talk to than others. It was advisable to have at least three pre-planned topics of conversation prepared for this ordeal – if they all drew a blank then you finished the meal in silence. The worst ordeal of all was to be placed next to the Headmistress at high table, something which required your very best table manners!

Table seating worked out well at those meals when we sat as six houses, but it was a problem at lunchtime, when we sat in nine forms with their numbers swelled by the inclusion of day girls. If you were not quick enough in bagging your seat, you were 'turned away' to another table. This caused much anxiety, although normally a kind girl on another table would see your predicament and offer you a spare seat next to her.

Teapots and milk jugs were in the middle of the table and whoever sat opposite was responsible for pouring the teas. Ordering one's preference was raised to an art form: watery weak, milky weak, no milk, milk-and-a-dash. Another girl would be in charge of cutting the bread (no sliced bread then) and a block of butter (more likely margarine) had to be meticulously divided into the correct number of portions.

Food was brought to the tables, and plates cleared away, by maids when enough could be recruited, otherwise we had to do it ourselves. One year we had Dutch maids, a group presumably recruited in Holland. They were young, friendly and wore pale blue dresses.

Various foods acquired special names. A solid sponge pudding baked in a cylindrical tin and served with red jam, or sometimes watered-down syrup, was Dead Man's Arm. If it contained currants, it became Dead Man's Arm with Squashed Flies and the end pieces known as Gym Shoe. Tapioca or sago was Frog Spawn. A green, rather soft blancmange was Green Phlegm Pie and semolina Pound Hill Slime (the local area). Bread – standard white –

arrived in double-length loaves which were pulled apart before reaching the table. The surface where the two halves had parted was called the Fly Walk and was considered quite a prize; one of the first sounds when talking was allowed was "Bags I the Fly Walk" – reserving this bit of the loaf. Equally, some girls would "bag" the crust. By far the most popular dish was Queen of Puddings which one of the more imaginative housekeepers somehow managed to produce.

Occasionally we would have kippers for breakfast or high tea, and whatever was next cooked in the same trays also tasted of kippers!

On Sundays the girls had to wash up after lunchtime, presumably to give the domestic staff some time off. This was done in a gloomy room containing two huge teak sinks which got very slimy (no Fairy Liquid or Marigolds in those days). About six girls at a time would be on washing-up duty, and we became adept at taking a big pile of plates, drying just the top and bottom and quickly stacking them away in the cupboards.

Food during the wartime and the years after must have caused the housekeeper many headaches. Raspberry jam, late 1940s style, was believed to contain tiny wood chips in place of pips to disguise the fact that no fresh fruit was involved. Some small boiled eggs tasted odd and we were told they came from Poland where the chickens were fed on fish meal. Meat was sliced very thinly and tended to be fatty; often the gravy was watery and grey. Scrambled egg was a solid mass swimming in liquid. Spam fritters were a staple, and also pilchards in tomato sauce. Sunday tea would always be something cold – occasionally 'Norfolk Rotation' which was shredded carrot, cabbage, beetroot and any other vegetable to hand, arranged in neat and colourful rows on a long tin platter. However it was the one day when we had cake, which was a treat.

There was a formal etiquette at mealtimes. You could not ask your neighbour to pass you something. She was expected to notice that you might need something and offer it to you. If not, you went without! In practice, however, a system of nods and nudges evolved, and even asking your neighbour if she would like something (even though it was obvious she didn't) in the hope she would then offer it to you. The reason behind this strange rule was presumably to encourage us to be good hostesses in the future.

Just outside the dining hall, in a small, pillared section of the original building, was placed a table and chairs at which girls studying French could sit with their teacher and speak French throughout the meal. This was known as French Table and later, when German classes started, also served as German Table or Deutsch Tisch.

Towards the end of the meal the bell would be rung for silence, which was the cue to hurry up and finish eating. We learnt to eat fast! The meal ended with a final grace and we filed out in an orderly manner and in silence.

There were a few special treats. In the summer, on Wednesday afternoons after games, we had ice cream. Sometimes in the evenings there was cocoa and perhaps jam sandwiches or bread and dripping.

A girl whose birthday occurred during term time could have a cake sent by her parents for sharing at teatime with her housemates. Shackleton House was particularly fortunate as the father of one of the girls was a master baker and his creations were spectacular. One year the cake was shaped like a basket, with a handle, and brimming over with very realistic fruits made of marzipan and icing. The poor prefect had the unenviable task of trying to cut it into suitable pieces. She then asked the girl "please could you ask your father to send a square cake next year?" He did.

Another girl's father was a fruit farmer and he would send pounds of strawberries in the summer – enough for the whole school to have a feast.

Looking back, school food was pretty dull and rather stodgy, but somehow the housekeeper managed to give us nutritious meals. We were not overweight (probably because we also exercised a lot) and we were rarely ill.

HEALTH AND WELLBEING

Just occasionally there was an epidemic of some kind. The Easter term of 1929 was the term of epidemics. First of all they had influenza, then a case of mumps and finally two cases of chickenpox.

In May 1953 (just before the Coronation) Miss Farrell sent this letter out to parents.

Milton Mount College, Crawley

15th May 1953

I much regret that yesterday four girls developed German Measles. In the ordinary course of events this would be a trivial matter, but in view of the approaching Coronation holiday it becomes important. Parents will realise that it will be possible for a girl to develop the disease while away from school, though I do not propose to prevent girls from travelling because of quarantine. Parents and hostesses may not be willing to receive them in these circumstances. If a girl has had German Measles before it is likely to give her immunity but not certain. It therefore seems right to give you full warning of this, and I myself will wish to know as soon as possible if girls are to remain at school. Unless I hear to the contrary by Saturday 23rd May I shall assume that the arrangements of which I have already been informed will hold good.

M.L.Farrell

In 1957, we also had a very severe epidemic of Asian Flu which affected a large number of us. This meant that school life as we knew it was curtailed until further notice since so many girls and staff were ill.

But on the whole we were pretty fit. In January each year we all had to see our own GP and get him to fill in a form to be sent to the school to say we were in a fit state of health. And at the beginning of every term we had to present ourselves to Sister or Miss Chapman (her deputy) to have our hair examined for nits. As far as we know, none were ever found! We were given cod liver oil and vitamin tablets at breakfast which kept us all reasonably healthy. When colds were prevalent there was salt water provided in all the bathrooms for us to gargle with.

One girl had a nasty accident on her arrival at school:

Shortly after arriving at MMC I scuffed my feet along the wooden boards in the corridor in my bedroom slippers. A 2½ inch strip of wood went into the ball of my foot. I still remember the violent dreams while under gas at the Crawley hospital where it was removed.

In Shackleton the house mistress had a thing about fresh air and when she came round at night to switch the lights out, she always made sure that there was a window open, whatever time of year it was. It didn't always stay open! But in the summer term it was a privilege to have a bed near to the open window.

In winter, however, the cold did get to us. There were radiators or at least hot pipes on the ground floor, but upstairs could get very cold and many of the girls suffered from chilblains – uncomfortable itchy swellings which affected the fingers and toes. These became even more inflamed when we had to go down to the music cells in winter to practise, so many of our mothers knitted gloves with half fingers to wear to keep our hands warm.

In the spring term of 1947, the big freeze, many girls had flu and so the whole school was sent to bed for two days.

Sister had dispensary every morning where we could go to get our throats swabbed if we had a sore throat or collect medicines if we had them prescribed. We lined up for nose drops to be administered when we had colds. She also ran the Sanatorium (called the San) where you had to go if you were really ill. An early prospectus says:

There is a resident trained nurse. One part of the building which can be completely isolated, with an outside staircase, is set apart for those who, for any reason, need the care of the Nurse.

None of us remembers the outside staircase.

The San was a large room with about eight beds in it. Fresh air swept in through open windows but it was never cold. Sister was in charge and kept a strict routine. When I had the Asian influenza bug for the second time we all had injections which after a week cured us. Sister believed all our ailments were due to constipation and gave enemas to remedy the problem.

This gave rise to many memories like the following:

When I had constipation Sister whacked a suppository into my backside and then sat me on a pot in the centre of the ward (humiliation to have to sit on a pot). Fortunately out popped the suppository to remain in the pot – all by its lonely self. Sister was furious and made me sit there until I performed.

One girl recalls:

The San was a place to be avoided, at least I thought so. It had a very definite smell, and visitors were not allowed. Instead we wrote notes to each other, left on the window ledge near the San to be delivered by Sister to the patients. Two naughty girls – I confess to being one of them – had learned from a teacher that if you sucked orange peel your temperature went up. We tried it and presented ourselves at the daily surgery, hoping to avoid a wet walk or something similar which we did not like by going into the San. Sister put us in a room in silence, but when meal times came there was no meal. She was not as naive as we thought. As the hunger began to hurt, we asked for food, but it was withheld for 24 hours. We did not suck orange peel again.

The San. I think I was 13 or 14 when I had German Measles at the end of the summer term. As German Measles did not make us, or me, feel ill, it was rather frustrating to be shut away. Time was passed by talking or reading. The San sitting room (known as San-sit) was a corner room I think, light and sunny, overlooking the Dutch lawn, and had a supply of books. The maids who came round to clean also chatted to us. Sister checked on us, temperatures and pulses, saying "Handy-Pandy Jack-a-Dandy - that's what I always say." No doubt she also enquired if we suffered from constipation.

We were an amazingly healthy lot. This was very largely because at every available opportunity we were outside or taking part in some activity.

CHARITIES AND EXTERNAL LINKS

B.H.L.

Barnardo's Helpers' League was supported by the school for many years. In the 1920s it was known as the Young Helpers' League and the school supported a cot for the care of a specific child. In December 1925 the bazaar in aid of the cot realised over £33 (about £1,800 in 2016). The cot was moved to Hove Convalescent Home and Matron kindly sent a postcard description of each new occupant until she left. Each form had a collecting box. The next year several girls went to Hove to see the child in the cot over which there was an inscription "Milton Mount Cot".

Each autumn there was a sale and a series of sideshows to raise money and the details were reported in The Miltonian. In the 1930s the sums raised averaged between £55 and £60 (over £3,500 in 2016).

In 1936 the Miltonian said:

"The B.H.L. Sale was held on 5th December and, as in previous years, proved to be a great success…. A stall which attracted much attention – as always! – was the 6th form sweet stall. In spite of the sarcastic remarks re smells, enticing or otherwise, issuing from the still-room during the term, the stall was cleared amazingly quickly by enthusiastic visitors and girls, thus rewarding the efforts of the diligent but often despairing cooks. The sideshows began about four o'clock, and screams and much laughter could be heard coming from the Upper 4th's Chamber of Horrors."

Post war, the takings seem to be about £70–£80. Who can forget the annual visit – started in 1947 – by the redoubtable Miss Ramsbotham, telling us the recent news from Dr Barnardo's? Not the most inspiring speaker, but there was no escaping the lecture.

At this time we "adopted" a child and she (Jean) received a beautiful doll in 1948 and a doll's tea set the next year. David was our next protégé and he lived in the Ifield Barnardo's Home. This enabled two senior girls to take him out for tea in Crawley on his birthday with a friend. David then chose a present. One year it was a model gliding set. The report noted that in 1958 David left the Ifield home and was in Lancing training to be a chef.

Canning Town

The East End of London always has been and still is one of the poorest in the UK. It has always had a transient population with its associated problems, and philanthropists in the late 19th century set up a series of 'settlements' based on religious principles which were designed to counteract poverty and promote education. One such was Canning Town Women's Settlement, founded in 1892, to which Milton Mount College gave continuing support. It spread over several locations in the deprived East End. Its purpose was promoting women's education and training, improving health care and caring for disabled children as well as improving working conditions. There were clubs for children and adults and a holiday fund to provide country holidays for deprived children.

The first reference to Canning Town at the school is in June 1929, when the Canning Town Settlement Dramatic Society performed 'Will O' The Wisp' and the last act of 'The Kingdom of God'. A netball team also came down and in spite of bad weather, a most exciting match was played. There is a report in 1951 about a visit from a party from Canning Town Settlement in July. "They arrived in time for school dinner and afterwards played energetic netball and rounders matches against the school, finishing up with a well earned swim and a picnic tea on the Dutch lawn."

There are no more reports in The Miltonian – the burgeoning of the Welfare State removed much of the need for Canning Town and other settlements after the 1950s.

There is, however, the above photograph in the archives captioned "Canning Town Brownies, 13th November 1954". This was taken on the steps leading from the tennis court area to the terrace. The steps are still there and replica urns have been installed.

Fen Place

The building at Turners Hill known to Miltonians as Fen Place had stood for around 300 years when it was converted into a home for retired Congregational ministers and their wives and widows. It had been a 17th century farmhouse and became associated with the Shelley family when John Shelley married the younger daughter of Roger Bysshe, of Fen Place. The building appears on maps of 1724,

1789–1808, and 1839–1840, and was owned by Sir Timothy Shelley, Bart, in 1842.

In the early 20th century the house and about 740 acres, including six farms, were owned by a director and governor of the Bank of England, Mr William Middleton Campbell. Herbert William Looker lived at Fen Place in 1930, and Commodore Hon Trevor T Parker DSc RN (retd) lived there between 1934 and 1938.

The house was used by the War Office during World War II, and by 1950 was empty, with smashed windows, ingress of rainwater and dry rot. The grounds were neglected. Largely through the influence of Rev Dr Maurice Watts (father of an Old Miltonian who attended MMC during the 1950s), the house was acquired by the Congregational Union in 1951, restored and used as a retirement home for the next 30 years.

Audience at a performance by girls from MMC, 1953

Between 1951 and the closure of MMC in 1960, senior girls visited Fen Place on several occasions; to sing carols at Christmas, perform plays or concerts, and to visit the residents.

Most notably, several were present when the late Queen Mother officially opened Fen Place on 8th July 1952 and planted a golden cupressus to commemorate her visit. Some of them were photographed with the Queen Mother. See the photograph on page 75.

Since 1984 the building has become the Alexander House Hotel (now five star), and extended over the years to incorporate a luxury spa. The Miltonian Guild has been fortunate enough to meet there for reunions in recent years, and on one of these occasions (2006) three of the girls present at the opening were photographed under the – now huge – golden cupressus.

The three former pupils with the 1952 photograph

DISCIPLINE

Discipline was strict, but usually fair. Houses competed for cups – Order, Tidiness and Deportment. The Order Cup was awarded to the house with the fewest disorder marks. These were given by either staff or prefects for such misdemeanours as talking at the wrong time or running along the corridors. You had to own up in front of your whole house that you had been given one and then go to the Upper 6th form room to be "squashed" (told off).

She would tell you that you had let down yourself, your house, your school and your parents who had sacrificed their all to send you to school. As a little girl I was never sure what 'their all' was.

One girl recalls getting an Untidiness Mark for leaving a pencil on her desk instead of putting it away.

Bad work or behaviour in lessons could result in being put in detention. This involved being sent to a basement room during your free time to complete some task, such as extra homework.

The most extreme punishment – for continued disobedience despite numerous warnings – was to be 'banished' from your house. This involved moving to another house for a week and being 'sent to Coventry'. Lessons continued as normal although your peers were not supposed to talk to you and at mealtimes you sat at a table alone. This was an appalling punishment and no one suffered it twice.

Being a naughty girl I learned a good deal about discipline and subsequent punishments. Sitting outside Miss Farrell's study putting string into luggage labels comes to mind, and I know the words of Isaiah Chapter 6 by heart to this day – learned as a punishment for something. The worst experience was to be called into the study and reprimanded for some misdemeanour or other and told that, as a minister's daughter, I should know better. I always found that hard to understand – and still do.

Breaking the Rules

We did not just learn from our academic studies but "tested the water" occasionally by breaking the rules, like any schoolgirl does. Getting up to mischief and, if caught, accepting the punishment, was all part of our training, but we did not always see it in that light then!

Below are some of the things we got up to, in no particular order.

Caterham School in Surrey was our "brother school". One year when the 6th form boys came over for a dance with the 6th form girls one girl, fully clothed, was thrown into the swimming pool. In the camellia walk a boy removed a fuse from the fuse box and, having plunged the area into darkness, tried to spike the drinks. A conga then started around the pond, and everyone danced into the building and up on to the roof. On the way down they went through one of the house dormitories and a horrified and furious house mistress was left holding the door while everyone trooped through.

A leaving party was held one night for a pupil leaving the Lower 6th. Those in the form not invited had tied cotton around the tables and chairs to try and trip up the others on their way to the French windows and terrace. They managed to get out and then into the swimming pool where they floated rather than swam as the Headmistress's house was nearby and she might have heard the noise coming from the pool. The leaver was a keen horse rider and she decided to go into the field so she could ride one of the cows.

On the way, by the lake, they woke up all the frogs who croaked so loudly they thought the whole school would hear the din. Fortunately the farmer had moved the cattle from the field, so there were no cows and everyone returned to their dormitories safely and undetected.

The bathrooms consisted of cubicles which were divided from each other by scaffolding and canvas. "Reverse hanging" from the steel poles was a common practice. But one day it ended badly when a girl fell off and went to hospital with mild concussion.

April Fools Day was an ideal opportunity for pranks. On one occasion kippers were put under the staff table in the dining room (how on earth did we get hold of kippers?) and another time everyone went into assembly without their hymn books. The Headmistress was not amused.

Another wheeze was trying to walk or sit on the rim of the round pond without being spotted by the Headmistress looking out of her study window and putting your names in her black book.

It was rare for a class to become unruly but, if it did, the Headmistress would arrive and give us a stern lecture. Occasionally she would tell us some confidential and personal information about the mistress in question. This was more effective than a mere ticking off and made us feel ashamed of our behaviour. We tried not to forget that the staff did have a private life.

One pupil who hid on a shelf in a cupboard for the duration of a French lesson ended up sitting outside the Headmistress's study to reflect on her shortcomings – a salutary experience.

In 1949 a group of girls had gone out of bounds among the rhododendrons one Saturday afternoon, when two policemen appeared. The girls ran off, but they had been recognised as Milton Mount girls. Back at school they were summoned to the Headmistress's study and then had to sit, separately, either outside the study or in the main corridor, where they would be seen to be in disgrace. The police had been searching for John Haigh, the acid bath murderer, who had a house in Crawley. The girls were soon allowed to go as it was thought that the fright was punishment enough. Haigh was hanged later that year.

When returning to school, if boys were in the next carriage the girls would hang out of the windows trying to communicate with them. In those days train windows could be fully opened.

Hair washing was allowed every three weeks but many washed their hair – so-called "wigging" – more regularly by accidentally slipping under the bath water.

Midnight feasts were a regular event at the end of term, particularly the summer term. Day girls would be bribed to bring in "supplies", often tins of diced mixed vegetables. One girl's mother cooked a piece of gammon and thoughtfully sliced it up. The difficulty was getting rid of the evidence and so it was necessary to eat absolutely everything up which created some odd mixtures. On one occasion we were forced to eat up evaporated and condensed milk – not a good combination. The staff must have known about these but, wisely, they turned a blind eye.

I remember a midnight feast with my friends in the main school. I was in Livingstone House and had to make my way under cover of darkness. I don't remember what we ate but I know that condensed milk featured quite heavily – eaten with a finger from the tin. My return journey turned out to be rather frightening. When passing the triangle of hedges I saw a ghost in white and floating. I returned to the Quad rather faster than I had left and pounded up the stairs – risking disturbing Miss Lodge in her room. Luckily she must have been sleeping pretty soundly and didn't hear me. I don't think I did it again!

Some girls were playing ball in the courtyard of the Quad when the Headmistress came to collect her car. They were told to go elsewhere to play, but they stayed there and were caught by her again as she returned earlier than expected. Their punishment was being sent to sleep in an empty dormitory alone each night for a week. Very scary.

Putting a pillow at the bottom of the bed and vaulting over on to the bed, gradually adding more pillows until the springs broke and the bed became more of a cradle – cosy when tucked in at night.

A pupil said that she wanted to go to the toilet during study time when she wanted to meet a friend in the corridor to help her with her Latin. The punishment that resulted was for telling a lie, not for helping her friend.

Two day girls argued at Three Bridges station, a school hat ended up scorched on the gas lamp, and homework on the railway line. Both were retrieved by the porters, but a new hat had to be purchased.

For a joke girls would pour cold water on a bath occupant but one day it went very wrong as scalding hot water was tipped by mistake, resulting in the unfortunate girl spending a week in the Sanatorium.

It was rumoured that Lady Montefiore's ghost walked in the camellia walk after dark. Some daring girls went at night to investigate, but never saw her.

Once a class imitated a teacher's Irish accent. They were told they could talk in their own accents, but no one else's. The next day they spoke to her in Yorkshire, Cockney, Welsh and Scottish brogues, and all ended up in detention.

A girl did a handstand on the tennis court whilst waiting for her friend to fetch some balls. She was spotted and sent to bed in silence. When her partner came to find her she told her what had happened and the unfortunate girl was immediately in trouble again for talking and had to sit in the main corridor at study time for two evenings

Poking a ruler behind a frayed tapestry wall hanging brought a rebuke that we should appreciate beauty.

Older girls were allowed to go to Crawley on Saturday afternoons. On one occasion cream horns were purchased, but this had been observed by the prefects. They were ordered to go later that evening to the prefects' room with their purchases. Prior to going, they ate the cream and filled the horns with white paste used to mark the lines on the tennis courts. When they arrived the prefects told them to eat the pastries – they must have known what the girls had done. They nibbled slowly, dropping bits surreptitiously, and were finally told to put the rest in the bin.

Bats used to live in the Quad and some girls, if they caught them, would keep them in drawers in the dormitories.

If money and sweets were not handed in when they should have been, and were found in drawers, not only was discipline enforced but a reminder given that "these two items near each other might poison you!"

Reading banned books with the wrong covers on them, sometimes in class, also got some girls in hot water.

Day girls had to wear their hats until they reached home.

One day I returned to school in the evening in school uniform minus my hat. I was reprimanded by the Headmistress, but explained that I had been home. Unbeknown to me, my mother was in the school at the time and the Headmistress was able to verify that what I had said was correct. She came to apologise to me, but the very next day a new rule came into force that hats were to be worn if outside the grounds in school uniform.

On the rare occasions when a man was seen in the school, this caused great excitement among the girls.

One girl recalls:

One day a member of staff was sitting in a deck chair on the staff lawn with her back to us. My friend and I crept out of bounds to the end of the camellia walk to see what was there. We thought we had accomplished our mission undetected. Almost 20 years later, when I met that teacher again, she calmly said "I knew what you were both up to behind me". A lot of harmless happenings were wisely overlooked. (Both my friend and I went on to become school governors).

The cricket-playing daughters mentioned in Chapter 8 were identical twins and seemingly hard for the staff to tell apart. Miss Farrell decided that the twins ought to be separated so that they might become more independent and make their own friends. Therefore one twin "stayed down" in the Lower 5th after their first year at MMC. After being separated, they decided that for one week they would swap over lessons and dormitories. Seemingly even their closest friends did not realise, and they were not found out for the entire week.

THE WAR YEARS

When the Second World War broke out, Miss Farrell was faced with the colossal task of blacking out the whole building. Girls of Livingstone House were moved into the main building and staff and girls painted skylights and domes black, cut up what dark fabric they could find to make curtains and fixed bits of black felt to the shutters where rays of light penetrated. In addition to this the timetable had to be completely reorganised to enable day girls to get home before dark. Despite the many problems, school life went on almost as usual until June 22nd 1940, when the War Office requisitioned the building as accommodation for Canadian soldiers. The school was given exactly a week to evacuate the building, which was achieved by moving most of the furniture to the Quad, with chairs in the music rooms and desks in the camellia walk.

Miss Farrell scoured the country for pos-sible premises to house the school, and finally secured a lease on the Imperial Hotel at Lynton in North Devon. Girls in Shaftesbury House lived in the annexe to the hotel and those in Raleigh House moved into a series of rooms over small shops. As the hotel had no grounds, games had to be played in the public park, the younger girls used a hilly field as their playground, and the public courts were used for tennis. The furniture was moved from Worth Park and the school term started on September 5th 1940.

In the bus which brought us from Barnstaple the excitement
increased. Soon the bus was climbing the steep hill to Lynton and
we had reached our new abode at last. Our first glimpse of it was

disappointing; from one side the hotel is hidden by shops and when we arrived a large furniture van was blocking the entrance. But on that first day the thing which impressed us most was the view from the windows. The bedrooms seemed very small and crowded at first, but this was soon forgotten in the novelty of wash stands with hot and cold running water and French windows opening on to balconies.

The Imperial Hotel

The days that followed have left me with many, varied impressions. One of the most vivid is of our first gym lessons in the Congregational Sunday School Hall. Several tiny Primary School chairs caused much amusement. The hall itself seemed very small and the floor unyielding after the first class gymnasium at Worth Park.

Pianos were to be found in all sorts of places such as the vestibule and linen room, while violinists had to gather what inspiration they might in a dormitory at the top of the annexe.

The friendliness of the people here has made a great impression on us. During those first few days we were continually stopped by people eager to welcome us and to express all manner of hopes for us.

Lynton was a small country town in which the girls could enjoy rather more freedom than at Worth Park. There was less emphasis on 'out of bounds' with free access to Lynton and to Lynmouth, the cliff railway, the zigzag paths and the Valley of the Rocks where wild goats roamed and wild bilberries grew. Girls could do their own shopping, and could bathe in the swimming pool at Lynmouth or at Lee Bay.

Longer walks could be taken to Woody Bay or to Oare in the Doone Valley. One girl recalls being chastised for being late back to school and was really upset because she thought she would be praised for walking 21 miles in less than five hours!

The girls could also take part in the life of Lynton, and gave performances to the public in the Town Hall, sometimes in aid of charity. The school could also play matches against Badminton School, from Bristol, which was temporarily housed in the Tors Hotel in Lynmouth. Joint lectures and concerts were also possible, including an oboe recital by Leon Goossens. The older girls cultivated an allotment and grew vegetables for the school.

Churchill House, home to girls of Raleigh

Here's an account of that time by a member of staff, now aged 93.

I joined the teaching staff of Milton Mount College in September, 1944. It was my first appointment on leaving Bedford College of

Physical Education. The school's main building was the Imperial Hotel situated near the top of the main road, a very steep hill, which led down into Lynmouth. There were several other buildings close by offering further accommodation for staff and pupils.

As far as P.E. was concerned, the venues where it took place were scattered throughout the small town, and I certainly got plenty of exercise taking classes to and from these as well as participating in them. Netball was played on what had been the local car park. Gymnastics took place in the Congregational Church Hall, just over half-way up the main street, and dancing lessons were in the Town Hall, about three quarters of the way up the main street. As for games – lacrosse and cricket were played in The Valley of Rocks at the far end of the town, sometimes it was so windy here, standing up could be a bit of a problem never mind trying to throw a ball about.

Tennis at Lynton

My accommodation was a flatlet on the top floor of what had been a bank, level with the church tower on the opposite side of the road, and when it was windy I was lulled to sleep by the flapping of the lanyards on the tower's flag pole! Another interesting feature was the fireplace. When I tried to light the fire the smoke not only came back down the chimney but out of the sides of the mantel-piece as well. The piece-de-resistance of the bedroom was a rope ladder under the bed which I was informed was the fire-escape! I was asked to test it – so I threw it out of the window and set off down it only to discover it finished about six feet from the ground, so I had to hold onto the final rung and drop off – interesting to say the least.

In the main hotel building near the entrance on the ground floor was the Staff Room which had been the hotel Secretary's office, one of the few places where there was a telephone. Sitting in there during a free period one morning the door flew open and in a great flurry came Miss Linton, the Housekeeper. She grabbed the 'phone, rang a number and I was astonished to hear her say "Is that the Fish Mongers? Have those kippers caught the bus?" I had a vision of the kippers, two by two, holding flippers and trotting down to the bus on their tails – and I burst out laughing but she was not amused!

I remember one day when there was a rumour that a German sub-marine was in the Bristol Channel, and the entire town shut down and many of the inhabitants set off along the cliff walk overlooking the channel. One man even took his gun along, but their vigilance was unrewarded – no sub appeared.

The end of the war in Europe occurred in 1945 and Lynton did its best to celebrate. We all attended a film show at the local cinema and were each given a small tin of ration biscuits, so hard we nearly cracked our teeth. The cinema machinery was somewhat out of practice and kept breaking down or running the film backwards, but the town officials had done their best to celebrate the coming of peace.

Some girls heard via the radio in the next room that the Second World War had ended. Wanting to put a note under the door of their friends' dormitory to tell them, but having no paper, they peeled off a piece of wallpaper and used that.

The whole school apparently also celebrated VE Day with a picnic in the Doone Valley.

Return from Lynton to Worth Park. Although Worth Park was derequisitioned in June 1945, the school had to remained at Lynton until April 1946 because of the extensive damage done to the building and the grounds by the Canadian soldiers. The Easter Holiday in 1946 was extended so that preparations could be made for the return of the girls, and the school eventually returned on 1st May. There were only four members of staff and about 25 girls remaining from those who had left so hurriedly nearly six years previously.

A different regime awaited. The school train left Victoria Station at about 4 p.m. Arriving at Three Bridges the cases were taken up to the school by van and we walked up the long drive for the first time.

We gathered in the beautiful Assembly Hall where Miss Farrell welcomed us. She said we could wander around the school grounds as we wished after tea. They were in a sorry state with several army huts dotted about. Some bore 'educational' drawings left by the soldiers.

At the next Assembly we were given instructions as to where bounds were. The ha-ha was the boundary. The lake was out of bounds, as was the maze. We who had missed out visiting these the previous evening were disappointed. The tennis courts were unplayable and the games field covered with ridges and holes. These were soon restored, as was the swimming pool.

At Lynton we had a very restricted building with no land but surrounded by wonderful rugged scenery with a backdrop of the sea and a distant view of the Welsh coast. We had the freedom of the town together with Lynmouth with the Cliff Railway, the zigzag path and the sea water pool. In contrast Worth Park had lovely, elegant grounds with a distant view of the lake and a beautiful building with plenty of space. The Dutch garden, the camellia walk, the round pond and the terrace were all features. For those who had been at Lynton quite a lot of adaptation was needed. According to Miss Hilda Harwood's 'History of Milton Mount', during the first term girls had to be excused lessons once a week to do essential cleaning and washing up.

The south terrace looking towards the camellia walk

On 10th May a special thanksgiving service was presided over by Rev Clifford Hall, Chairman of the Governors, and addressed by Rev F Chalmers Rogers, Chairman of the Congregational Union. Miss Farrell was given unstinted praise for her leadership during the war years.

Many of us were very sad to leave Lynton, which had been a beautiful and tranquil place during the dark days of war. As Miss Farrell said "It is a joy unspeakable to be coming home, and to feel that we can begin the constructive work of restoring the school to what it was."

THE JOURNEY TO CLOSURE, AND BEYOND

When you are a small schoolgirl and a ceiling falls on to the Deputy Headmistress, without causing injury, hilarity ensues. However, unbeknown to us at the time, it was the beginning of the end of the school at Worth Park.

There was no compensation for the damage caused by the Canadians in the Second World War. Milton Mount College was an independent school with no grant aid; many pupils were daughters of Congregational ministers who were admitted on a very low fee scale and there was no endowment fund. There was therefore no money to carry out any necessary maintenance and, in addition, the Governors considered that the nearby growth of Crawley New Town, and Gatwick Airport, made the area no longer suitable for a girls' boarding school, and new premises would need to be found.

Plans were submitted to the Crawley Urban District Council for the site to be sold and developed as a residential area. Permission was not granted, and the Ministry of Town and Country Planning upheld the Council's rejection. An alternative scheme was embarked upon, but was also unsuccessful.

The Board of Governors met in April 1960. Until then they had never contemplated closing the school but they were now faced with an insurmountable cash flow problem, and a Headmistress soon to retire. Consequently, just two days after the Board meeting, all the parents were informed that the school would close in July that year.

Should the school have ended in this way? Some of the pupils' parents and alumni were princes, ambassadors and missionaries and some of the Old Girls had become national names. Had they been asked, and given time to organise financial support, the outcome may have been very different. It was hoped that an opportunity might arise to reopen the school.

The closure of the school had severe implications for girls part-way through their secondary education. During the last term they found themselves doing entrance exams for their prospective new schools – all the time hoping that no more ceilings would fall on them.

In July, each girl was asked to choose a book from the library, and parents began arriving to purchase the pictures, garden urns etc. that were being sold.

It was customary for 'Auld Lang Syne' to be sung on the last day of the summer term around the round pond. In 1960 we did not get very far before the singing ended with everyone in tears.

> This had such an impact on me that I vowed there and then that if it was ever in my power, I would never let a school close again. That opportunity would come years later, as you will discover further on in this journey.

Some of the pupils went to Wentworth College in Bournemouth, with which Milton Mount College was to merge in 1962. The income from the small Bursary Fund, trust funds and sundry other money was used to support these girls and some others who needed help to further their education.

Milton Mount College had closed its doors, and pupils had dispersed to various schools in this country and abroad. But a new phase in the journey was about to begin, which kept the ethos alive. This is evidenced by the Milton Mount Foundation, Bournemouth Collegiate School (now BCS), Worth Park Gardens, the archives in the West Sussex Record Office, the Miltonian Guild, and this book. All of them, apart from the Miltonian Guild, will still exist long after the last Old Girl has gone.

The Milton Mount Foundation (MMF). This was set up in 1967 to administer the proceeds from the sale of the buildings and grounds. This money was invested in a Fund (a registered charity), drawn up by the Congregational Union of England and Wales in consultation with the Ministry of Education. The income is used for bursaries for the education of ministers' daughters from the Congregational Church (now United Reformed Church).

URC ministers can apply to the Fund for help towards the payment of school fees, uniform and books at URC-related schools for their daughters and, now, their sons. Only the income from the capital can be used for this, and the aim is to support the child throughout its school life.

Regular URC attendees may also apply, as may adults studying ministry-related subjects. Bournemouth Collegiate School applications have priority and if – after all approved bursaries have been allocated – funds remain, some may be given to the parents of Foundation pupils to assist with the cost of their extra-curricular activities.

Bournemouth Collegiate School (now BCS). In 1961, once it was apparent that Milton Mount College could not open again, negotiations began to merge with Wentworth College in Bournemouth which was a similar girls' boarding school with a few day pupils. The merger finally took place in 1962 and the school became known as Wentworth Milton Mount.

Over time money was given or loaned by the Milton Mount Foundation and Miltonian Guild to provide additional facilities for the school, such as a huge multi-purpose hall, new music block, additional science rooms and a large indoor swimming pool.

In July 2008 it became clear that history was repeating itself. The school was in serious financial trouble and receivers entered the building. Nobody knew whether the staff would have jobs by the start of the autumn term, whether the pupils would have a school to return to, and whether parents therefore needed to look for new schools for their children.

This is when I had the opportunity to put into practice the vow I made in 1960, never to let a school close again.

The United Schools Trust agreed to purchase the school, and the doors re-opened in September 2008. The Trust is now called United Learning and has a portfolio of profitable schools which funds the purchase of a failing school until it becomes viable. The President of United Learning is The Rt Rev and Rt Hon The Lord Carey of Clifton, former Archbishop of Canterbury.

During the last 20 years the school's name has changed several times and in 2016 it became, simply, BCS. It is now a co-educational school with pupils aged two to eighteen, with boarders, flexible boarders, and day students. The prep school is in Poole and the senior school in Bournemouth.

Worth Park Gardens. Once the school had closed, the grounds became very neglected but were later taken over by the local Council. A Britain in Bloom judge, when being shown round the gardens, said it was an ideal place to build houses. Ironic, as that is what the governors had wanted in 1960.

It was time to act. The Friends of Worth Park was formed in order to submit a bid to the Heritage Lottery Fund to re-establish the gardens. It was unsuccessful. Another group was formed – The Worth Park Friends – and they were encouraged to re-apply, this time for a Historic Heritage Lottery Grant. This was successful, and in December 2011 over £2 million was awarded for restoration of the gardens over a five-year period.

The large Pulhamite urns had been sold in 1960 but, through the Milton Mount archives in the Record Office, it was possible to trace someone who had an original urn from which authentic replicas could be produced, and these are now in place.

A Steering Group was set up consisting of representatives from the local Council, project managers, expert professionals, and a former pupil of the school. The Council has to undertake to continue to maintain the grounds after the initial five-year period ends in December 2016. The official opening day was in July 2015 with the fountain working again and over 2000 visitors attending.

The fountain back in operation at last

The gardens have been entered for various awards. In both 2015 and 2016 they achieved a Royal Horticultural Society silver gilt award by South and South East in Bloom. In July 2016 the gardens were given a Highly Commended Sussex Heritage Award in the

Public and Community category (sponsored by Gatwick Airport Trust) "to recognise and reward high quality conservation and restoration."

The Heritage Lottery funding period ends in December 2016, and a final project was needed to utilise the remaining available money. In fact it has been possible to initiate two.

Firstly, the remnant of a cedar tree blown down in the gardens by the autumnal gales in 2015 has become the expertly carved Timeline totem. This has a stag's head at the top above the Montefiore shield, below which the school is represented by books on a bookshelf with an owl sitting on it, and then some camellias, with a cow at the bottom to commemorate the farm and its dairy.

Secondly, a group of Jersey cows (which the Montefiores bred and indeed won prizes for), carved from old oak from the Parham estate, will be sited just beyond the ha-ha. An information board will explain the purpose of the ha-ha.

The Milton Mount Archive. This is held at the West Sussex Record Office in Chichester. We have our own Old Girl archivist, and a designated member of the Record Office staff, who between them catalogue our artefacts which are still being sent for deposit. The catalogue is therefore professionally compiled and maintained, easy to use, and forms a unique, permanent and secure record.

This Book. When it was suggested that boarding school experiences should be documented while former pupils were still alive there was a lot of enthusiasm and the book evolved. It has been hard work but fun to do and will provide yet another legacy of our years at Milton Mount College. The Record Office has accepted all the submissions.

The Miltonian Guild. Founded in 1888, the Guild is open to both staff and pupils who were at Milton Mount College. We also welcome the Head of BCS together with a representative from each Head's era. Even now, in 2016, we still have over 150 members worldwide.

Reunion at Wentworth Milton Mount, October 1977

We have an annual reunion based near our old grounds, spending time in the grounds or at activities based on school life. On the Sunday we attend Worth Church, and our Guild Prayer is read out. In 2000 a very successful reunion was held in Lynton. Once a year the Committee meets in London to catch up with everything. The Regional Secretaries keep in touch with their area members and often hold local reunions.

Reunion in May 1988 to celebrate 100 years of the Miltonian Guild

At the start of each year all members await our outstanding colour magazine. Everything stops while it is read from cover to cover. As some of the Miltonians are not able to travel far now, it is an important way to keep us all connected.

The 2004 tree planting

A liquidambar tree was planted in the grounds by the Mayor of Crawley in 2004. A plaque below it commemorates the school. The Montefiore rooms in the Quad, which were refurbished under the Historic Heritage Lottery Fund, contain a clock and a barometer given by the Guild. These were presented at our opening ceremony for the restored gardens in May 2015 when the Mayor of Crawley unveiled them (her husband had planted the tree). The Mayor also read one of Lady Wilson's poems which related to the school (reproduced on page 136).

We are indeed privileged to have experienced being at such a school, which in later life we realised had taught us so much, even if we were not aware of it at the time.

The journey to closure was not the end. The ethos of the Founders is still alive and will go into perpetuity.

LASTING EFFECTS

To girls of the 21st century boarding school life must appear tough at best and even archaic at worst. It is interesting that in the contributions received for this book homesickness is rarely mentioned. This was, of course, a fact of life especially among the younger girls, but usually it lasted for the first term only. After the first holiday at home, girls were eager to return to all their new friends at school. A downside of being sent to boarding school is the lack of friends in the home environment and the necessity to rely on siblings, family and any school friends who lived near enough. Parents would often invite a particular friend of their daughter to stay with them for a while during the holiday, and this could be enormous fun.

Another fact of school life which has not yet been mentioned was the practice of having "crushes" on members of staff or older girls. This was totally innocent and was more a matter of seeking a role model than anything else. For some obscure reason we termed it as being "gone on" someone. Games mistresses were usually chosen because they tended to be younger than other staff members as well as being fit and better looking. Sometimes an attractive member of the 6th form might be the subject of such adoration.

In spite of the magnificence of the building, MMC was a small school which allowed it to be quite intimate, and the cosiness of the house system was effective in making us feel at home. There was a great sense of family and pulling together.

Although we were mostly confined to the school grounds, we had plenty of freedom with many opportunities to explore and enjoy the grounds. Indoors, too, there was much to occupy us.

The magnificent building welcomed us, as if it woke up at the sound of young footsteps and happy chatter.

There was plenty of room for personal development and, however small your talent, a place was always found for it to be nurtured. Overall, there was still time to be a child and there were nights when whispered conversations went on long after 'lights out'.

Although, by today's standards, we were extremely innocent, we did learn to stand on our own two feet and be independent. Living and working together was a vital area of development.

It was expected that we would have a career and ultimately be able to look after ourselves, but that we didn't have to be particularly academic or clever to get on in the world.

The education, in retrospect, was less than brilliant – most leavers were not Oxbridge material – and careers advice extremely sketchy.

I remember my time at MMC with great affection – loving all the opportunities for sport and having friends around me. The ethos of the school has remained with me all my life and for that I am grateful.

Our education gave us the skills to work things out for ourselves, so even if you were not academic you still had the basics for achievement and an attitude of "can do...." It certainly helped me a great deal in my working life.

I made some lovely friends and the strict attention to behaviour did me no harm.

One of the most valuable outcomes from those years was the insight into a world shared by people from many different backgrounds. Girls regularly flew out to where their parents lived and worked.

Brazil and Kuwait I remember and, increasingly in the years I was there, girls from other cultures.

A forward-looking and inspirational school.

It formed the basis of my Christian faith and thus gave me a pattern as to how to live my life.

Whether we liked it or loathed it, and there are those who would admit to both, we were privileged to be there and cannot help being influenced by the Christian ethos which we lived and breathed. The basic principles of compassion, selflessness, honesty and respect were part of our daily living and we must surely admit to taking these qualities into our later lives. We learned from the staff, especially the Head, not only by words heard but by lives lived. Yes, we learned independence and resilience, but also survival which has sustained many girls through challenging adult lives.

The open-minded Christianity learned was, I think, ahead of its time and whether or not we have retained the faith we had, we have benefitted from the experience of being part of the Miltonian community.

The friendships and experiences, music and laughter, assemblies and so much else that is still part of me I owe to my time at Lynton and even more at Worth Park. I am delighted that the grounds are now properly cared for.

EMINENT MILTONIANS
(Maiden names first. If married – married name in brackets)

Dr Elizabeth Jane MOFFETT 1866–1960

Gained MD at the London School of Medicine in 1894. Worked in school medical service in Staffordshire and Birmingham. From 1916–1919 she was attached to the Royal Army Medical Corps. In 1911 her property was sold at Stafford market owing to her refusal to pay taxes in the Votes for Women campaign!

Alice J BATER 1866–1952

One of the first women to qualify for a BA.

Dr Maud Mary CHADBURN, CBE, MD, BS 1868–1956

One of the first women doctors to qualify. Consulting surgeon to the Marie Curie Hospital and South London Hospital for Women and was responsible in a great degree for their foundation.

Catherine B ROBINSON, MBE 1869–1951 (Mrs A W Alderton)

She was alderman, magistrate and the first woman Mayor of Colchester; an ardent politician and distinguished president of the Women's National Liberal Federation.

Edith Emmeline STARMER 1869–1948

Ran a successful art studio in Mundesley, Norfolk, with her brother, Walter Starmer.

Eveline M FARREN, JP, LLD 1870–1956 (Mrs Lowe)

Joined the staff of Homerton College, Cambridge, becoming Vice Principal before her marriage to Dr G C Lowe, a distinguished London physician. First woman Chairman of the London County Council in 1939.

Ethel Louie STARMER, MB, CM 1871–1965 (Mrs O'Melvena)

Qualified as a doctor in Edinburgh in 1897. Went out to China under the United Presbyterian Missionary Society. She escaped the murderous attacks on the Mission at Moukden in 1900. As well as using her medical skills, she lectured to both men and women in the college.

Edith CALVERT 1877–1956 (Mrs Turner)

School Captain in 1896. Became matron of the Women's Hospital in Wuchang, Central China. After her marriage to Robert Turner they went to Papua. She was the first woman to be admitted to the Papua District Council and first woman Chairman.

Marjorie LEGG, FSAA 1896–1985

Qualified as a chartered accountant in 1925, one of the first women to do so.

Evelyn HAILE, MBE 1900–1994 (Mrs Burns)

Outstanding maternity work in Serowe, Botswana. She was devoted to her "babies".

W Alice NEWCOMBE, MBE 1901–1992

LMS missionary in Samoa and Tutuila; came home to look after her mother. Her MBE was awarded for 60 years service to the Girls Brigade.

Truda UFFEN, OBE 1904–1995 (Mrs Bishop)

Founded a club for ex-prisoners in Leicester and wrote a book about it 'They All Come Out'. Became a magistrate in 1945 for which she received the OBE.

Margaret Teify RHYS 1906–2001

Studied history at Newnham College, Cambridge. It was not until 1948 that the authorities agreed to confer proper degrees on women. She famously coxed the first Cambridge women's boat to row against Oxford. After the war she became an inspector of schools in various parts of the country.

Dr Joan THOMPSON 1909–1973 (Mrs Bryson)

One of our distinguished medical women, whose service with Dr Howard Somervell at Neyyoor Hospital, South India, will long be remembered. She was an obstetrician and gynaecologist. She retired to Worthing where another old Miltonian once consulted her at the local Family Planning Clinic.

Nina Warner HOOKE 1910–1994 (Mrs Thomas)
Author of 'Seal Summer'. Wrote full length comedies and one-act plays.

Grace PARRIS 1911–2010 (Mrs Richard)
Qualified as a pharmacist in 1933. Edited 'The Years Between' 1926–1939, the period of Mrs Henman's headship. Secretary of the Miltonian Guild 1955–1964. She gave a large quantity of archives which are now deposited in the Record Office.

Joan CORKE, MBE 1914–1995 (Mrs Glover)
Spent some years in Hong Kong as Secretary and Housing Manager to the Hong Kong Housing Society, for which she received the MBE.

Marjorie ("Bunty") WHITE 1914–1995 (Mrs Bates)
Solicitor in 1938 specialising in criminal and matrimonial practice. A formidable advocate and is believed to be the first woman solicitor to appear regularly in the Isle of Wight Magistrates Court. Hon Legal Adviser to Miltonian Guild 1950–1995.

Gladys Mary BALDWIN 1916– (Mary Wilson, later Baroness Wilson of Rievaulx)
A Congregational minister's daughter, she went to MMC in 1928 and left in 1932. She married Harold Wilson on 1st January 1940 at Mansfield College Chapel, Oxford.

A poem 'Eventide' was printed in the 1929 Miltonian magazine and 'My Night Adventure' in 1930. She has had books of poems published, 'Mamzelle' being read at the May 2015 Reunion (and reproduced in this book). Her husband was Prime Minister

1964–1970 and 1974–1976. He was knighted in 1976 and created a life peer in 1983.

Anne LAMB, OBE 1918–2010
In 1972 she was Deputy Chief Nursing Officer for the Department of Health & Social Security and was awarded the OBE for services to nursing. She wrote a seminal book on nursing.

Patricia (Pat) BOHN 1922–1998
Worked for the Civil Service. In 1943 she was selected to be part of Winston Churchill's mission to the "Big Three" conferences in Cairo and Teheran. She joined UNESCO in 1947 and retired in 1982, but remained in Paris. Left £30,000 to the Miltonian Guild in her will.

Mary BRENCHLEY 1924–2000 (Mrs Dick Francis)
Wife of Dick Francis, the jockey and author. Her memorial service was held at the Queen's Chapel of the Savoy in London.

Alison C SHRUBSOLE, MA, CBE 1925–2002 (Mrs Hilton Brown)
Principal of Homerton College, Cambridge 1971–1985. Previously senior lecturer at Stockwell College, London and from 1957 founding principal of Machakos Teacher Training College in Kenya, which she and her pupils built up from scratch.

Rosalind GRIFFITH JONES, JP 1927–2008 (Mrs Goodfellow)
Moderator of the General Assembly of the United Reformed Church 1982–1983. Taught history before her marriage. Chairman of the Free Church Federal Council 1997–2001. In the 1990s she was chair of the governors of Wentworth Milton Mount in Bournemouth.

Elaine KAYE 1930–2015
Headmistress, Oxford High School 1972–1981. Lecturer in Theology (Church History), Mansfield College, Oxford 1996–1999. President, URC History Society 1997–2002. Author. Gave the

address at Miss Farrell's Memorial Service in 1979. She helped to found The Adam Von Trott Memorial Appeal. Adam, who studied in Oxford in the 1930s, became a central figure in the plot to kill Hitler and was put to death in 1944. The Appeal, launched in 2004, works to strengthen understanding between Germany and Britain, and provides a scholarship to bring young German students to Oxford. Elaine received the Cross of the Order of Merit of the Federal Republic of Germany in recognition of her contribution.

Anne GEAR 1938–   (Mrs Buckingham)
Anne was awarded the MBE in the New Year Honours list 2011 for "services to beekeeping in Surrey".

Sylvia HOLDER 1938–   (Mrs Hann)
Winner of The Times/Sternberg Active Life Award 2012 for her dedication to improving the education of children in Kovalam, Tamil Nadu, South India. Sylvia set up The Venkatraman Memorial Trust in 2004 and is still actively involved in its work which has included the building of a 1000-pupil high school.

Extract from 'The Years Between' 1926–1939:
Looking back, it is interesting to realise that all walks of life have had Miltonians in their ranks – Doctors, Dentists, Pathologists, Pharmacists, Almoners, Singers, Actors, Musicians, Teachers, Secretaries, Civil Servants, Members of Parliament with Cabinet rank, Local Government Officers, Librarians, Justices of the Peace, Lawyers, Bankers, Nurses, Probation Officers, Missionaries, Ministers of Religion, Magistrates, Head Mistresses, College Principals, owners of Independent Schools, Farmers, Shopkeepers, the three Armed Services – in fact "you name it, we've done it" – and at the time of this article (1975), a Prime Minister's wife.

MAMZELLE

By Mary Wilson
Reproduced by kind permission of the author.

The Summer Term had just begun;
My desk was warm beneath the sun;
I leaned across the window-ledge
To smell the springing sweet-briar hedge.
The quiet garden seemed to wait;
I heard a footstep by the gate,
Across the grass a shadow fell —
I looked, and saw Mamzelle.

My mouth is dry as she goes by —
One curving line from foot to thigh —
And, with un-English liberty
Her bosom bounces, full and free;
Pale skin, pink lips, a wide blue stare,
Her page-boy fall of silky hair
Swings on her shoulders like a bell;
O how I love Mamzelle!

She cannot get her idioms right,
She weeps for Paris in the night
Or, in the tension of the Match
She laughs when someone drops a catch!
The other staff are not unkind
But distant; she tries not to mind,
And I would gladly go through Hell
Just to protect Mamzelle.

On Conversation Walks we go,
I touch her sleeve – she doesn't know;
All summer's beauty round her lies
As 'Parlez français, girls!' she cries.
I do not smile, I do not talk,
In silence by her side I walk
And hope that no one there can tell
How much I love Mamzelle.

The sunny days are hurrying past;
Their painful sweetness will not last;
The poppies burn among the hay,
The heartless cuckoo sings all day;
The Home Farm woods are green and cool,
There's laughter from the swimming-pool.
At end-of-term I say farewell
For ever, to Mamzelle.

Perhaps I shall forget her face,
Her gentleness, her body's grace;
Even her accents, deep and slow,
May be forgotten. And I know
That I, throughout the coming years
May love with joy, may love with tears;
But shall I ever love so well
As now I love Mamzelle?

Mamzelle with four girls

INDEX

140

Blazer badge, sports colours and a well-worn tie

Classmates reunited in June 2006

The Timeline Totem

Original Miltonian Guild badge